GARY RAILWAYS
by James J. Buckley

International
Standard Book Number 0-915348-84-5

Bulletin 84 of the
Central Electric Railfans' Association,
an Illinois not-for-profit corporation
P. O. Box 503, Chicago, Illinois 60690

Issued May 1949
Enlarged Edition, August 1975

Printed in the United States of America

Foreword

Gary, Indiana, is at the lower end of Lake Michigan, 26 miles southeast of Chicago. Sometimes called the "workshop of America", the Calumet region within 16 miles of the center of Gary encompasses 25% of the steel production in the country and includes the largest single steel-producing facility, that of Inland Steel Company at Indiana Harbor. Altho the region's local transportation is now by bus, the city was once the center of several interurban and local street railways. People could travel from Gary to La-Porte, Chesterton, Valparaiso, Hobart, Crown Point, and Hammond on interurban cars operated by Gary Railways, Inc., or its predecessors. While Gary's last street car has given way to the rubber-tired vehicle, its links with the east and west are still by electric railroad service of the Chicago South Shore & South Bend Railroad.

The purpose of this bulletin is to tell the complete story of Gary Railways, Inc., from its beginning in 1908 to the cessation of street car service in 1947. Every effort has been made to make this story as complete and accurate as possible. This could not have been accomplished without the kind cooperation of Mr. F. M. Kemp and Mr. J. W. Davies of Gary Railways, Inc.; it was only thru their patience and tolerance of our endless questions that all this material became available. We also wish to thank Mr. Ernest Sohn of Hobart, without whose fine memory we should never have untangled the story of Hobart operations. Much material was also checked against the standard references, including Electric Railway Journal, Poor's Public Utilities Manuals, and "Air Line News", published by the Goshen South Bend & Chicago Railroad. A special effort was made to obtain complete photo coverage, and again we must thank Messrs. Kemp and Davies whose files produced some of the most interesting items. Finally, a vote of thanks to all the others who have borne with us in making up this bulletin.

History of Gary:

The transportation problems of Gary are perhaps a little more understandable with a quick study of Gary's history.

As the nation entered the twentieth century, the demand for steel and its finished products began to climb rapidly, exceeding the capacity of the older eastern plants. After considerable study of various locations, the United States Steel Corporation selected the northern Indiana site as being ideally located with respect to materials, market, labor and transportation, and named it Gary after Judge Elbert H. Gary, Chairman of the Board of that firm.

In the spring of 1906, construction of the Gary works was begun by a subsidiary, the Indiana Steel Company. The plant consisted of blast furnaces, open-hearth furnaces, iron and steel foundry, rail mill, plate mill, merchant-bar mill, billet mill, car-axle plant, large slabbing mills, and a by-product coke plant. By the end of 1911, most of these mills were completed.

Adjoining the Indiana Steel Company to the west another subsidiary, the American Sheet and Tin Plate Company, was built. This comprised modern sheet and tin plate mills of large capacity, which process large slabs and bars from the Indiana Steel plant. South of the Tin Plate mill was located the new American Bridge Company plant, built after U. S. S. acquired this fabricator of large structural jobs.

U. S. S. organized Carnegie-Illinois Steel Corporation in 1935. The Illinois Steel Company (successor to operations of Indiana Steel Company) and American Sheet & Tin Plate were merged into Carnegie-Illinois. Further corporate simplification occurred in 1951, when Carnegie-Illinois and American Bridge were merged into U. S. S. The Gary steel-producing activities are thus now part of the Central Division of U. S. S., while the bridge fabrication maintains its identity as a separate division.

Background of Gary Railways:

CHICAGO - NEW YORK
ELECTRIC AIR LINE RAILROAD:

Altho in April 1906, Gary was non-existent, this date was the beginning of the Gary electric railway system. At this time, the Goshen South Bend & Chicago R.R., more familiarly known by the holding company name, Chicago-New York Electric Air Line R. R., was incorporated. According to its promoters, the route chosen between Chicago and New York was to be 742 miles in length, shorter than any steam railroad. Passengers would be carried between terminals in 10 hours for a fare of $10.

THE AIR LINE:

Fabulous tales have tended perhaps to overemphasize the importance of the Chicago - New York Electric Air Line Railroad, which was, after all, a jerkwater streak of rust that went from noplace to nowhere and hadn't enough traffic to keep two small cars busy. But the imaginative, if impractical, plan of its promoters kept the road in the forefront of possible sources of private investment capital.

Top: Car 102 with very heavy load enters LaPorte about 1908.

At left: Car 101 drifts lazily westward to temporary Westville Road terminal. (Two photos, Van Dusen-Zillmer collection)

Lower left: Car 101 noses out of South LaPorte carhouse, 1908. At the time, only the center track was in use. (Stephen D. Maguire collection)

Bottom: This kind of operation couldn't hope to stand on its own feet. Belatedly, lines were built to points where there were potential passengers. This crowd at "Valpo" welcomes the first car on the Valparaiso & Northern Railway, July 4, 1910. (G. Krambles collection)

Construction was started in September 1906 at LaPorte. After much ballyhoo and constant pleas, for more money, five miles of line between LaPorte and South LaPorte were put into operation on June 15, 1907. Over 2000 people rode the line on that historic day, and enthusiasm for the project ran high.

Building an absolutely level railroad across the rolling Indiana countryside proved to be no easy task and it wasn't until November, 1911 that a 15-mile tangent was finally completed between South LaPorte and a point where a junction was made with the Valparaiso & Northern Ry. This junction was named Goodrum, after G. C. Goodrum of Fall River, Massachusetts, a heavy investor in Air Line shares.

VALPARAISO & NORTHERN RAILWAY:

The Valparaiso and Northern Railway was incorporated in August, 1908 as a feeder to the Air Line. It was to connect both Valparaiso and Chesterton with the Air Line and was controlled by the GSB&CRR thru 51% stock ownership. Three miles of line were opened July 4, 1910 between Valparaiso and Flint Lake, a well-known resort spot. Two second-hand cars, plus excursion trains of saddle-tank locomotives pulling flatcars from the construction equipment, fitted with benches, handled the 3500 curious people who rode on opening day.

The section between Chesterton and Goodrum was put into operation on February 18, 1911 and service then offered by a bus between Flint Lake and Goodrum. The latter was replaced by cars when the railway was completed up to Woodville on October 7, 1911. When a bridge over the Baltimore & Ohio Railroad at Woodville was opened on February 17, 1912, thru operation became possible between Valparaiso, Chesterton and LaPorte.

GARY CONNECTING RAILWAYS:

In order for either GSB&C or V&N to make any appreciable earnings, it was imperative to make a connection promptly into Gary. To accomplish this, a new company, the Gary Connecting Railways, was incorporated in June, 1911 and immediately leased to GSB&C, owner of all of its stock. The line was completed between Gary and East Gary in sub-zero weather and operation was begun by the Gary and Interurban Ry. on January 6, 1912. By August 5, 1912 track was completed between East Gary and Woodville, a junction with the Valparaiso & Northern Ry. The formal opening of this section of line took place August 14, with the participation of city, town and county officials of the territory served. This was the occasion for the first, and probably the only, thru train between Hammond and South Bend, via LaPorte and the Chicago South Bend and Northern Indiana Railway. Three cars took part. On September 5, 1912 regular service began between Hammond and LaPorte, with connections to Valparaiso and Chesterton.

GARY AND INTERURBAN RAILWAY:

Immediately after securing a franchise, Frank N. Gavit organized the Gary and Interurban Railway, with papers of incorporation issued in July, 1907. The contract for a complete street railway system was let to the Co-operative Construction Company, which had done all other Air Line work. Work began on Broadway in December, 1907.

Provision for the car lines was made in the original layout of Gary. A median strip was left in paved streets on which it was planned to build car lines. Such streets were Broadway from one end of town to the other, and crosstown, Fifth and Eleventh Avenues.

The first street car to run in Gary left Jefferson Street car barns on May 20, 1908. Service began on Broadway between 22nd and 4th Avenue, where a viaduct was being built for the B&ORR. A later extension brought the line to the city limits at the Little Calumet River. Late in 1908, the 11th Avenue line was completed to Tolleston limits, with the intention of extending on to Hammond.

This extension was delayed by inability of the G&IRy to secure a franchise thru Tolleston, since the Chicago Lake Shore & South Bend Railway, which ran cars for about a year, held exclusive rights here. In the summer of 1909 G&I finally won the franchise from the Lake Shore, on the ground that the latter's service was unsatisfactory.

The Hammond franchise called for cars to be in operation by December 31, 1909. Construction began at once from the end of the 11th Avenue line at Gary and on Sibley Avenue in Hammond. Due to the severe early winter, it proved impossible to meet the deadline, but a car purchased from the Denver & Intermountain Railway was placed in temporary shuttle service out of Hammond until the line was opened for thru service on February 8, 1910.

EAST CHICAGO STREET RAILWAY:

The Air Line organized the East Chicago Street Railway to reach the Inland Steel Company plant at Indiana Harbor, which was employing some 4000 people in 1912. When completed on February 15, 1913 to a connection with the 5th Avenue line, the route was leased to the G&IRR for operation.

GARY & INTERURBAN RAILROAD:

Air Line stockholders began a movement in 1911 to purchase the Gary & Interurban Railway, and by February, 1913, 40% of its stock had been purchased with funds raised by the sale of 4% collateral bonds.

A new company, the Gary & Interurban Railroad was formed as a consolidation of the Goshen South Bend & Chicago R.R., the Gary Connecting Rys., the Valparaiso & Northern Ry., and the Gary and Interurban Ry. The first two were Air Line properties and the third was under Air Line control.

During 1913 several extensions were made to the Gary city lines. One new line was built on

In the early years the various "interurban" divisions each had distinctive equipment. Built for the Denver and Intermountain line, car 20 was diverted upon completion to the Valparaiso & Northern and ran for some time carrying the lettering shown. It ultimately became #404 of Gary & Valparaiso Railway. Next, the Valparaiso line used heavy steel "submarine" cars whose round end contours were typical of Kuhlman construction around 1918. (Both photos, George Krambles collection)

Left: The gas car did not find a congenial home on Gary Hobart & Eastern. The railway resorted to secondhand conventional trolleys.

Below: Rolling stock for Gary & Southern was more traditional, altho arch roofs on passenger cars were unusual in 1912. Photo of the then-new car was made at Lottaville barn.

Bridge Street from 5th Avenue to the American Bridge Company. Trackage rights on the Gary & Southern Traction Company's line on Broadway from the Little Calumet River permitted extension to 45th Avenue, about two miles each way. Construction began on a line from 145th and Main Streets on the Indiana Harbor line to Kennedy Avenue on the Hammond line. Numerous steam railroad crossings were involved, delaying the job, but the route was opened in March, 1914.

FRANCHISE DIFFICULTIES:

One of the conditions under which Frank Gavit was granted a franchise in Gary was that after five years the local fare would be 10-tickets-for-a-quarter or straight 3¢. Despite numerous protests the city remained adamant, and this, coupled with the rise of jitney cabs, brought on receivership. On December 1, 1914 G&I failed to meet interest payments on Gary Connecting bonds and on January 1, 1915 defaulted on all obligations. On October 17, 1915 a bill was filed in the U. S. District Court for foreclosure of the first refunding mortgage of the Gary & Interurban and Charles A. Davidson was appointed Receiver.

A new franchise granted in 1917 called for separation of the Gary & Interurban Railroad into its constituent parts. In return for a share of future net profits, the city granted a new 30-year franchise and revoked the old 50-year rights with their associated three-cent-fare clause.

Altho the city required the separation of all lines east of Broadway, bringing the GSB&C, V&N and GCRys back to life, there was no objection to the combined operation of lines west to Hammond and Indiana Harbor by the Gary & Interurban.

Five bidders bought the tracks, rolling stock, real estate and all other assets at upset prices fixed by the court at a Receiver's sale September 18, 1917. The Goshen, South Bend & Chicago Railroad, with 21 miles, two motor and three trailer passenger cars, capitalized at $7 million, sold for $75,000. Gary Connecting Railways, with 16 miles, two passenger and one express motor car, capitalized at $900,000, was sold for $50,000. Valparaiso & Northern Ry., with 12 miles, three passenger motor cars, capitalized at $600,000, was sold for $40,000. Gary & Interurban Ry., with 22 miles, 28 passenger motor and two service cars, capitalized at $2 million, was sold for $200,000. East Chicago Street Railway was sold to the Gary Street Railway for $125,000.

GARY STREET RAILWAY:

The Gary Street Railway succeeded Gary & Interurban. Gary & Valparaiso Railway succeeded Valparaiso & Northern and leased Gary & Connecting Railroad, successor to Gary Connecting Railways. Goshen, South Bend & Chicago and Chicago-New York Electric Air Line passed out of existence quietly with a simple notice in the papers stating that from November 3, 1917, service would no longer be given from Woodville to LaPorte.

In spite of seasonal heavy traffic to resorts on Flint Lake, the Valparaiso line remained a losing venture and its bondholders wished to take advantage of high scrap prices to get some return on their investment by scrapping the line. After a three-year fight, the people of Valparaiso saved the line by raising enough money to buy the line from the bondholders. A shuttle car continued operation from Woodville to Chesterton until 1922, when it was replaced by a bus.

A new line was opened by the Gary Street Railway on Buchanan Street in 1918, connecting the American Sheet & Tin Plate Company plant with 5th Avenue. In April, 1924 a line via 5th, Virginia and 2nd was opened to the newly-built National Tube Company plant. In November, 1924 the 5th Avenue line was extended eastward to Miller to serve the new municipal beach there. In the same year service was discontinued from East Chicago to Hammond via Kennedy Avenue, as unprofitable.

GARY & HOBART TRACTION COMPANY:

Until 1924, the Gary & Hobart Traction Company was independent of other Gary companies.

The first attempt to connect Gary and Hobart with an electric railway was the Gary, Hobart & Valparaiso Traction Company. Ground was broken at Hobart on May 14, 1909 and some bonds were sold after a short piece of track had been graded, but the promoters were unable to interest further capital in the plan.

U. P. Hord and J. B. Price of Aurora, Illinois, organized the Gary Hobart & Eastern Traction Company. Part of its five-mile right-of-way was donated. A gas-electric car was obtained from the General Electric Company and put into service on September 21, 1912. There was considerable trouble with the car, and after a month it went back to GE and later ran in Minnesota.

After suspending operations for two years, bonds of the road were pooled and, with the financial assistance of Aldia T. Ewing of Chicago, the line was electrified. Formal opening took place on May 3, 1914. Upon securing trackage rights over Gary & Interurban, between 37th Avenue and the mill gates, direct thru service began between Hobart and Gary.

The company was thrown into receivership after one year and was sold to Mr. Ewing and William Earle of Hobart in the spring of 1917. The new company incorporated under the name of Gary & Hobart Traction Company.

GARY & SOUTHERN TRACTION COMPANY:

The Gary and Southern Traction Company was incorporated in 1908. Work started in 1909 but very little was done until April, 1911. In January 1912, cars began running between the steel mills in Gary and the town of Lottaville, a distance of eight miles. The southern extension to Crown Point was pushed rapidly and was formally opened to traffic July 1, 1912. By 1922, jitney competition was so severe that officials of the company seriously considered abandonment.

The Family Tree

Column headings (railway lines): Crown Point line · Hobart line · Indiana Harbor line · Hammond line and Gary car lines · Gary-Woodville · Chesterton-Valparaiso · Goodrum-LaPorte

Gary & Interurban Railway Co.
- 7/18/07 -- Incorporated
- 5/20/08 -- Opened Broadway car line (4th Av. to 22nd Av.)
- 1908 -- Extended Broadway car line to Little Calumet River
- 1908 -- Opened 11th Av. car line (Broadway to Tolleston)
- 1909 -- Opened service within Hammond
- 2/8/10 -- Opened thru service to Hammond via 11th Avenue

Valparaiso & Northern Railway
- 8/25/08 -- Incorporated; controlled by and leased to Goshen, South Bend & Chicago Railroad Co.
- 7/4/10 -- Opened Flint Lake - Valparaiso (3 miles)
- 2/18/11 -- Opened Chesterton-Goodrum (2.5 miles)
- 10/7/11 -- Opened Woodville-Flint Lake (4.5 miles)
- 2/17/12 -- Opened Goodrum - Woodville (0.6 miles)

Merged 1/28/13

Chicago-New York Electric Air Line Railroad
(Holding company) Incorporated 10/1905

Goshen, South Bend & Chicago Railroad Co.
- 4/16/06 -- Incorporated
- 6/15/07 -- Opened LaPorte - South LaPorte (4 miles)
- 6/1908 -- Opened South LaPorte-Westville Road (8 miles)
- 11/1/11 -- Opened Westville Rd.-Goodrum (8 miles)

Merged 1/28/13

Gary Connecting Railways Co.
- 6/1/11 -- Incorporated; owned by and leased to Goshen, South Bend & Chicago Railroad Co.
- 1/6/12 -- Opened Gary-East Gary (5.5 miles)
- 8/14/12 -- Opened East Gary-Woodville (10.2 miles)

Merged 1/28/13

East Chicago Street Railway Co.
- 7/23/12 -- Incorporated
- 2/15/13 -- Opened Indiana Harbor-Gary (9 miles)

Leased 2/28/13

Gary, Hobart & Eastern Traction Co.
- 1/27/11 -- Incorporated
- 9/21/12 -- Opened Gary-Hobart (5 mi.) with gas-electric car
- 11/1912 -- Suspended service
- 5/3/14 -- Reopened with electric cars

Sold 3/26/17

Gary & Southern Traction Co.
- 4/25/08 -- Incorporated
- 1/1912 -- Opened Gary - Lottaville (8 miles)
- 7/1/12 -- Opened Lottaville-Crown Point (6 miles)

Gary & Interurban Railroad
- 1/28/13 -- Incorporated
- 1913 -- Opened Bridge Street car line
- 1913 -- Extended Broadway car line to 45th Avenue via Gary & Southern Traction Co. tracks
- 3/1914 -- Opened Hammond-Indiana Harbor via Kennedy Avenue

Separated into components 9/18/17

Gary & Interurban Railway Co.
- 9/18/17 -- Regained existence

Sold 9/26/17

Gary Connecting Railways Co.
- 9/18/17 -- Regained existence
- 11/19/17 -- Leased to Gary & Valparaiso Railway Co.

Sold 7/20/20

Valparaiso & Northern Railway
- 9/18/17 -- Regained existence

Sold 11/19/17

Goshen, South Bend & Chicago Railroad Co.
- 9/18/17 -- Regained existence
- 11/3/17 -- Discontinued LaPorte-Goodrum

Gary & Hobart Traction Co.
- 3/26/17 -- Incorporated
- Prior to 1924 -- Discontinued east of 3rd & Main, Hobart

Leased 10/1/28

Gary Street Railway Co.
- 9/26/17 -- Incorporated
- 1918 -- Opened Buchanan Street (Tin Mill) car line
- 1924 -- Discontinued Hammond-Indiana Harbor via Kennedy Avenue
- 4/1924 -- Opened Tube Works car line
- 11/1924 -- Opened Miller car line

Merged 8/15/25

Gary & Valparaiso Railway Co.
- 11/19/17 -- Incorporated
- 4/30/22 -- Discontinued Chesterton-Woodville

Gary & Connecting Railroad
- 7/20/20 -- Incorporated; leased to Gary & Valparaiso Railway Co.

Sold 8/15/25

Merged 8/15/25

- 1924 -- Midland Utilities Co. gained control of underlying companies
- 6/1932 -- Chicago & Calumet District Transit Co. gained control from Midland Utilities Co.

Gary Railways Co. Incorporated 8/15/25
- 6/17/33 -- Discontinued Gary-Crown Point
- 3/19/39 -- Discontinued Gary-Hobart
- 1932 -- Discontinued Coke Plant-Tube Works
- 1935 -- Discontinued Miller car line
- 1/29/38 -- Discontinued Sheet Mill-Tin Mill
- 3/19/39 -- Discontinued Indiana Harbor-Gary west of PRR station on 5th Avenue
- 1940 -- Discontinued Bridge St. car line
- 1940 -- Discontinued Buchanan St. car line
- 1/1941 -- Discontinued 5th Avenue car line (Broadway to PRR station)
- 1942 -- Reopened Coke Plant - Tube Works
- 10/23/38 -- Discontinued Garyton-Valparaiso (15.9 miles)
- 1/25/42 -- Discontinued Gary-Garyton (7.4 miles)

Reorganized 1/1/43

Gary Railways, Inc.
- 1/1/43 -- Incorporated
- 8/21/46 -- Discontinued Gary-Hammond
- 8/31/46 -- Discontinued Broadway car line (North Broadway to 45th & Grant)
- 2/28/47 -- Discontinued Tube Works car line (last railway operation)

All references in the Family Tree are to railway operations.

However, it should be noted that the property was one of the pioneer operators of motorbuses. Local service was inaugurated in 1922 on 8th Avenue, and intercity service reaching as far as 63rd Street, Chicago, followed in 1926. The intercity bus operations were transferred to Shore Line Motor Coach Company and passed from Gary Railways' control in 1931. City bus service remained "in the family" until the 1970's, when the Gary Public Transportation Corporation was formed to municipalize the remaining operations.

This pass was valid on all rail lines, as the exceptions named on it had been replaced by bus routes.

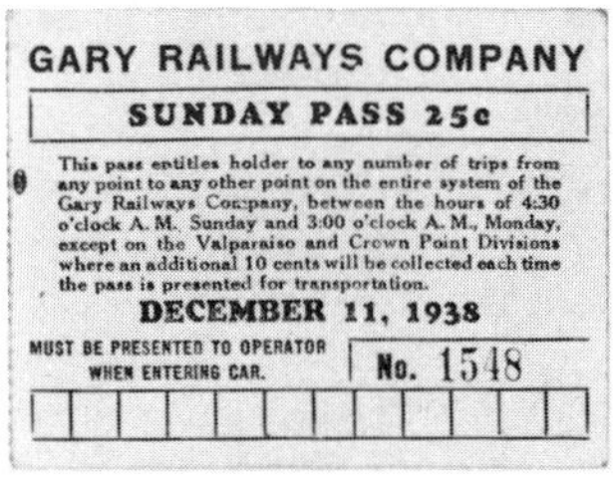

GARY RAILWAYS COMPANY — SUNDAY PASS 25c
This pass entitles holder to any number of trips from any point to any other point on the entire system of the Gary Railways Company, between the hours of 4:30 o'clock A.M. Sunday and 3:00 o'clock A.M. Monday, except on the Valparaiso and Crown Point Divisions where an additional 10 cents will be collected each time the pass is presented for transportation.
DECEMBER 11, 1938
MUST BE PRESENTED TO OPERATOR WHEN ENTERING CAR.   No. 1548

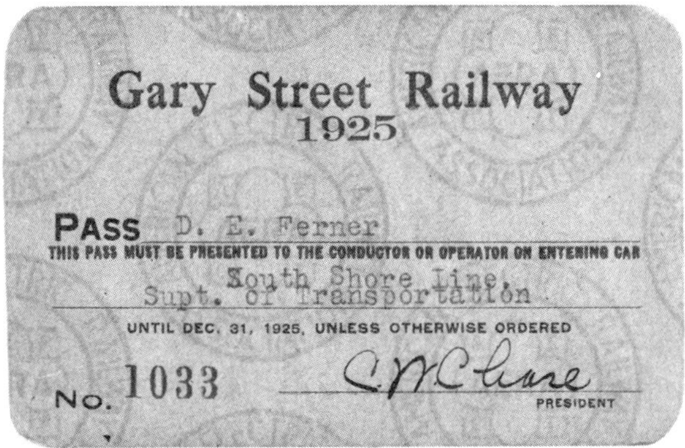

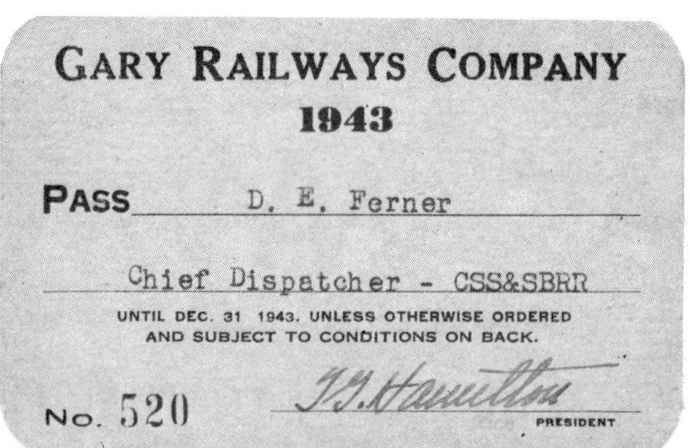

In October, 1928, the Midland Utilities Company purchased Gary & Southern and then leased it to Gary Railways.

Immediately after this a big improvement program was launched. An investment of $120,000 was made in new cars, substation and track. The new substation was built at Lottaville and further improvements in power were effected by additional feeder connections with Gary Railways. The track and pole line all the way from 45th Avenue to Crown Point was completely rehabilitated. The new cars, Gary's only single-enders, were modern, wide-observation, interurban type. Their comfortable, roomy, bucket-type seats were attractively enhanced with cool white seat covers.

The combination of improvements brought a sharp upturn in business to the Crown Point line, an increase of 100% being noted at the end of the first year.

GARY RAILWAYS:

Gary Street Railway, Gary & Connecting R.R., Gary & Valparaiso Ry., and Gary & Hobart Traction Co., all came under control of the Midland Utilities Company in 1924. Midland was an investment company engaged in public utility control thru majority stock ownership. As a result of Midland's activities, Gary Railways was formed in 1925 as a consolidation of the underlying companies.

Physical Characteristics:

TRACK:

The Goshen, South Bend & Chicago; Valparaiso & Northern; Gary Connecting; and Gary & Hobart all originally used 60 lb. rail. In 1926 the Valparaiso and Hobart lines were relaid with 85 lb. rail. Most of the trackage in Gary was of 85 or 90 lb. rail. The Indiana Harbor line was built of 85 lb. rail and the Crown Point line was built of 70 lb. rail which was replaced by 85 lb. stock in 1929.

POWER:

Originally, both GSB&C and G&I generated their own power. The Air Line had a power plant at South LaPorte and G&I had a steam station in back of their car barn at 22nd & Jefferson in Gary. Later it was found cheaper to purchase power and both generating plants were abandoned prior to 1912. Power was then purchased from Northern Indiana Gas & Electric Company, later from Calumet Gas & Electric Company. Since 1926, all power companies in the area have been acquired by Northern Indiana Public Service Company, from whom Gary Railways purchased its energy.

Substations of 300 kw. capacity were located at South LaPorte, Door Village, Woodville, East Gary and Lottaville; 500 kw. units were located at Cline Avenue on the Hammond line and at 37th Avenue on the Hobart line; a 1000 kw. unit was at Aetna on the Miller route, and a 2000 kw. station on 11th Avenue in Gary. A station on Third Avenue, owned by the city of Gary, fed the Tin Mill and Tube Works lines. All other stations were owned by Gary Railways, except Woodville and Cline Avenue, which were Public Service. The original sub at Woodville was destroyed in an electrical storm of the 1920s and replaced by an automatic. The original East Gary sub was destroyed by fire just prior to that, and replaced only by portable sub 2001 until the Aetna station on the Miller line was tied in to the Valpo line by a cross-country cable. A portable sub was also in use at Lottaville prior to construction of the new one in 1929.

CAR BARNS:

A combination power house and car barn was located at South LaPorte and a similar building was located at Lottaville. A wooden barn was located at Goodrum to house Valparaiso & Northern cars, while Gary Hobart & Eastern built their barn at Hobart, opposite Lake George. The corrugated iron car shed at Valparaiso was erected in 1927 to replace the Goodrum barn. The largest barn and main shop building was at 22nd & Jefferson in Gary. Originally built in 1892 as the first factory building in the area, it was purchased in 1907 by Gary & Interurban and remodeled into its new use. The building was then enlarged to double its former size. In 1941 it was again doubled to accommodate a modern bus garage, and in 1946 the building was completely remodeled to care for the conversion from rail to bus operation.

Financial:

Of all Air Line properties the only profitable one was Gary & Interurban, which paid dividends from its beginning until its merger with V&N and GSB&C. The latter were losing money and never had paid a dividend, and this added load coupled with franchise difficulties caused the company to lose money every year from 1913 thru 1917. The reorganized Gary Street Railway made money in each year but 1920.

Gary & Valparaiso made $129 in 1921, but was in the hole for losses ranging from 1920's $5000 to 1923's $19,723 for all other years except for 1918's happy $6000 profit.

Gary & Southern and Gary & Hobart ran along thru the years on a shoestring, with either a small loss or profit for each year. The Crown Point line had an unusually bad year in 1924, when it piled up a $13,764 loss.

The new Gary Railways Company did very well from 1926 to 1930, despite the slump which began in the steel industry in 1928. Under their management the property was entirely rehabilitated and each year a surplus was laid away.

ON THE HAMMOND LINE:
Above: Eastbound 200-class car at substation near the west boundary of Gary. (James J. Buckley)
Top left: Westbound at Ivanhoe siding, entering the city of Hammond, May 9, 1937. (John F. Humiston)
Left: Car 9, eastbound at Kennedy Ave. siding along 165th St., Hammond, 1945. (Stephen D. Maguire)
Below: The typical spring switch siding layout with Nachod block signal. (James J. Buckley)

Left: Rounding the curve, westbound at 165th and Summer Streets, Hammond, May 9, 1937. (John F. Humiston)
Bottom left: Gary car 14 at end of line, Hammond. Chicago Surface Lines #6204 passes in far distance, running on track of the Hammond company. (Ed Frank, Jr.)
Below: Looking east along 9th Avenue, Gary, on side-of-road flatland right-of-way so typical of Gary Railways ''interurban'' lines. (John Driver)

In 1932 the Chicago & Calumet District Transit Company acquired control of Gary Railways Company from Midland Utilities Company, and this year was also the worst in Gary's financial history. It wasn't until 1941 that Gary Railways was able to earn anything on the investment and in 1941 the controlling interest was taken over by the Bondholders' Committee. Wartime revitalization of Gary's industry brought prosperity to the company so that dividends could be declared for the remaining years of rail service.

Operation and Equipment thru the Years:

AIR LINE, 1907-1917:

Air Line interurbans operated thru from LaPorte to Hammond, using the typical big arch-windowed combination baggage-passenger cars numbers 101-104 (later Gary & Interurban 400-403). Air Line had an agreement permitting it to route its cars via any G&I lines, but Hammond was a more likely looking terminal in those early days than Gary.

Running time between LaPorte and Hammond was 2:30, including a 15-minute layover at Gary. Cars were scheduled to make connections with Indiana Harbor, Crown Point, Hobart and Broadway local cars in Gary.

When thru service was first begun there were eight regularly scheduled daily runs and nine on Saturday and Sunday. This was reduced by 1916 to six runs in each direction, which service remained until the end in 1917.

Shuttle cars operating between Chesterton and Valparaiso connected with Air Line trains. Until the 1913 merger, V&N cars 101 and 102 were used in this service; later they were replaced by the regular G&I 101-119 class. In addition to the Air Line cars, some runs were scheduled thru between Valpo and Gary, and for this service an odd combination car, V&N #20, was often used. This car was the one mentioned earlier which was acquired in a hurry from Denver and became known as the "Rocky Mountain Express" as it carried its original paint job and lettering until repainted in 1914. It then became G&I 404.

One morning and evening tripper also operated directly between Chesterton and Gary without change.

In Gary the main interurban station was at 11th Avenue and Broadway; in LaPorte, Air Line cars used the Chicago South Bend & Northern Indiana Railway depot and in Hammond, Chesterton and Valparaiso nearby stores served as ticket offices and waiting rooms.

On the run between Hammond and Gary, the interurban cars ran as limiteds, making the run initially in half an hour, with four stops. Later this time was lengthened to 45 minutes. Local service here was furnished with G&I equipment on a half-hour headway.

The Air Line had a serious accident on January 1st, 1916. This was a headon collision between cars 400 and 3000 at Brooks siding, near Westville. The motorman of passenger car 400 had orders to meet work extra 3000 at Brooks. Operating in a dense fog, he thought he saw the work train in the siding and continuing on, his car was telescoped by the high-wheeled 3000. Three people were killed and twelve injured.

Interurban cars were usually operated as single units but excursion business to two amusement parks required trailer operation. These parks were built by the company, one at South LaPorte and one near Clark Road. One of the trailers purchased for this service eventually ended its career in city service as number 500, while the other two were converted into milk trailers.

When used as passenger trailers, these cars were unusual in having a brass rail down the middle aisle for the convenience of standees and of the conductor in working thru the swaying car collecting his tickets. On one occasion some 225 people were packed into one trailer.

HAMMOND LINE, 1917-1946:

It has already been mentioned that, in addition to the thru interurban cars, local service was given in the early days by Gary & Interurban Railway, using the 105-108 type cars. These locals terminated at 4th & Broadway in Gary.

After the interurbans were taken off, service was furnished by various cars of the 101-128 group until 1922, when 120-128 were completely rebuilt and converted to one-man operation for the Hammond line. In 1927 nine new cars, numbered 9, 11-18, were assigned, and with the exception of the help of other rush hour trippers, these cars furnished all the service on this line until the end of rail service in 1946.

Prior to 1926 a regular run in the rush hours used trailer 500, obtained from the Air Line.

In early days, Gary cars operated in Hammond around a loop north on Calumet, west on State, south on Hohman and back east on Sibley. Later, sometime in the 1920s, this was changed to a stub-end at Sibley and Hohman, and still more recently, another block was cut off to eliminate a grade crossing of the Monon Railway.

Headway was originally 30 minutes with a 15-minute interval from Gary to Tolleston. In 1927 this was changed to 20 minutes thru and, during rush hours six days a week, 10 minutes to Rutledge Street, Tolleston. During the depression the old setup returned but with Tolleston cars running all day and evening to the end of double track. World War II brought a restoration of the 20-10 combination. Commonly runs were arranged so that a car made a trip from North Broadway loop to Hammond and return, then Tolleston and return, repeating this cycle all day, with additional trippers filling in to Tolleston and even to Clark Road during rush hours.

For the trippers, cars of the 109-128 class were used until 1937; from then on, 200-class were so assigned.

IN HOBART: Car 4 at 3rd & Main, the end of the line, 1938 (John Driver)...Early days at the carhouse with Gary & Hobart #2 (later #5) and ex-Chicago #2316 looking out (Frank E. Butts collection)...

TUBE WORKS LINE:
Left: Coke Plant station, end of the line during most of the 1930's...Right: #207 emerges from one of the underpasses (James J. Buckley)...Below left: The same car leaves the plant for the public street (John F. Humiston)...Below: #207 yet again, rumbling east along a deserted 2nd Avenue on Saturday noon, June 18, 1938 (Robert V. Mehlenbeck)...Below right: #206 on 5th Avenue, approaching Massachusetts Street westbound, on the section once shared with the Miller car line (Thomas H. Desnoyers photo from Norman Carlson).

Gary & Southern Traction Co.

Leave Crown Point A. M.	Leave Gary A. M.
5:25	6:30
6:25	7:30
7:30	8:30
8:30	9:30
9:30	10:30
10:30	11:30
11:30	P. M.
PM	12:30
12:30	1:30
1:30	2:30
2:30	3:30
3:30	4:30
4:30	5:40
5:30	6:30
6:55	8:00
9:00	10:00
10:00	A. M.
	12:35

CROWN POINT LINE:
Left: From GRys 1927 timetable (Benedict collection)...At right: #51, built for this line, on the city segment after the interurban was abandoned. Dash sign indicates destination street (William Baier)...Opposite page: #50 at the Erie crossing near Crown Point (G. Krambles).

...One of the newer cars entering Hobart by the causeway thru Lake George (John F. Humiston)

HOBART LINE, 1914-1939:

Hobart cars operated from the beginning directly to the main gates of the big steel works at the north end of Broadway. Originally projected toward Valparaiso, the line was unable to get its tracks across the Pennsylvania Railroad at Hobart, altho it operated to that point for many years. Prior to 1924 the line was cut back to 3rd & Main in Hobart.

Cars ran on a 90-minute headway until 1925, using two St. Louis cars in base service, except that a Birney car operated in base service from 1920 to 1923, when it was sold.

Trippers were run at shift change times of the steel mills, and it was on these runs that the big wooden number 7 proved most useful. It was able to carry 25 people in the front vestibule alone. In 1925, light weight cars 4 and 5 were assigned to this line with 200 and 120-class helping out as trippers. All of the older cars were then scrapped.

As a result of one motorman's insistence, car 213 operating on this line became the only one of the 203-218 group to have its headlight on the roof instead of on the dash like its brothers.

TUBE WORKS LINE, 1924-1947:

This line served the Coke Plant of the Carnegie-Illinois Steel Company and the National Tube Company, another U.S. Steel subsidiary. At first a 30-minute service was maintained using certain thru-routed Bridge Works cars. Later, continuous all-day service was dropped; only trippers ran as needed. National Tube prohibited the use of automobiles on their property, except for certain official cars, and Gary Railways thus had the job of moving 2500 people twice daily. The problem was solved with the use of trailers. Trains ran south on Broadway to 26th Avenue, where they could be turned.

The Tube Works shut down completely in the depression of 1932 and service was cut back to the Coke Plant. Trailers were discontinued but all other types of cars saw service. The line had several underpasses below railroad tracks and the dips in the street car tracks at these points had become so rough that it was impossible to keep fenders in repair and they had to be taken off all the 200-class cars for use here.

During World War II service was extended back to the reopened Tube Works. Now cars ran only as far south as 5th & Broadway, where transfer connections were made to all other routes.

CROWN POINT LINE, 1912-1933:

Crown Point cars terminated in Gary at North Broadway loop, but no passengers were handled locally between there and 45th Avenue. Only two cars were required for the 55-minute run, meeting on a single-end siding opposite Oak Hill Cemetery. After Gary Railways modernized, Gary & Southern Traction continued in classic form with the last two-man cars on any Gary street. Upon unification of management in 1928, these cars were replaced, at first with one-man cars from

THE FIFTH AVENUE LINES:

Right: Car 8 at the end of the Indiana Harbor line, Guthrie Street, the terminal of three competing electric railways many years earlier. (J. Driver)

Below: Running alongside Cline Avenue, an Indiana Harbor car en route to Gary crosses the Calumet River (John F. Humiston)--

Below right: --and bumps across the superelevated rails of the South Shore Line. (William C. Janssen)

Above left: Another South Shore Line crossing was on the Bridge Street branch. (John F. Humiston)

Above: Passing a Hammond car in Indiana Harbor.

Left: Car 6 southbound on the Indiana Harbor division enters the left side of 141st Street siding on March 18, 1939. (John F. Humiston)

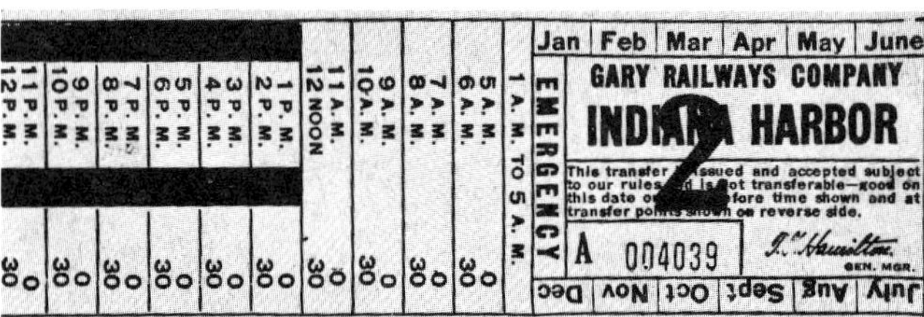

ALONG BROADWAY:
Numerous turnback points closely fitted the service to the demand in each section.
1-#27, on a 40th Avenue trip, has just passed the South Shore Line station. (Robert W. Gibson)
2-#22, en route 45th & Broadway, crosses 5th Avenue on July 4, 1937 (William C. Janssen)
3-Hobart car follows city car. (R. V. Mehlenbeck)
4-#20 at 45th & Fillmore. Only "45 Grant" cars served this section. (William C. Janssen)

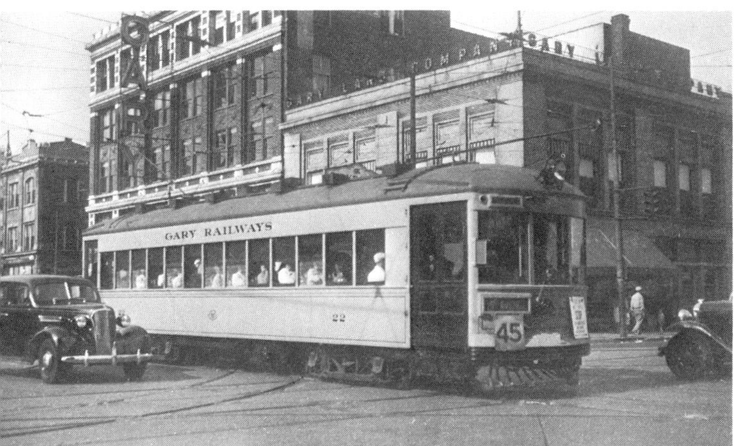

the other interurban divisions. The following year two modern one-man lightweight deluxe cars, Gary's finest, numbers 50 and 51, were substituted. Service continued to be hourly.

INDIANA HARBOR-FIFTH LINE, 1913-1941:

Indiana Harbor cars originally terminated in Gary at the interurban station at 11th & Broadway, but not long afterward they started switching back at 5th & Broadway and continued to use this street terminal till street car operation was discontinued in 1939.

Originally serviced by the workhorse 109-128 group of cars, the line got some help in the twenties from 201 and 202. Then in 1926 came the 6-10 class.

Headway was hourly until World War I, when service was made half-hourly and continued at this frequency thruout the life of the line.

Fifth Avenue in Gary was served by a combination of the Indiana Harbor, Bridge Street and Tin Mill lines. In the 1930's the latter two routes were operated on a 15-minute headway each and were so scheduled to give a $7\frac{1}{2}$-minute service to Fifth Avenue. Cars of all types, including Birneys, were used. Trippers with trailers ran from the Tin Mill to 26th & Broadway at mill shift times. Some runs cut back at Bridge Street without going out to the American Bridge Company (Ambridge) plant.

The Tin Mill line was shortened to the Sheet Mill in 1938 and was taken off altogether, along with the Ambridge line, in 1940. However, service on Fifth between Broadway and the Pennsylvania Railroad depot continued until 1941.

The Pennsy station was the scene of a disastrous collision between brand-new car number 9 and car 201. The wreck occurred in a dense fog and somehow the trolley came down and set both cars afire. Neither car could be salvaged. Another new car was purchased to replace #9.

BROADWAY LINE, 1908-1946:

Base service on Broadway was maintained by 101-128 type cars up till 1919.

Shortly after the G&I reorganization, the increasing cost of labor and materials, combined with the ever-growing competition of buses and private autos, began to offset the advantages of serving one of the fastest-growing cities of the country. The first attempt to relieve this situation was made February 2, 1919, when eight Birney cars were placed in service on Broadway between the mills and 26th Avenue. Headways were reduced from $7\frac{1}{2}$ to 5 minutes. In the rush hours, $3\frac{1}{2}$-minute service was given with the help of some two-man cars. The service improvement won cooperation of city officials, and soon an ordinance excluded jitneys from Gary's streets.

Shortly thereafter the new Peter Witt type cars arrived to replace 101-128 on Broadway thru-line base service. Cars 109-119 continued to work the street in rush periods, pulling trailers on three routes terminating at 26th Avenue loop. These routes began at the Tin Mill, the Sheet

ALBUM OF THE VALPARAISO DIVISION:
(All by John F. Humiston, 1938)
1-Crisman. 2-East Salt Creek. 3-Meet of trains 30 (car 2) and 35 (car 3, in distance) at Esserman. 4-The memorable cut at Wahob. 5-Wahob siding. 6-Long Lake. 7-Long Lake trestle. 8-On the curve from Flint Lake down to Long Lake.

Mill and at North Broadway loop.

The new 19-27 type, which by coincidence came in 1927, replaced the Peter Witts in the Broadway base, and these in turn, after being revamped to conventional floor plan, moved down to replace the 109-119 pulling trailers in the peaks.

In 1932 the single-door Birneys (numbers 701-710) were retired, altho the double-door single-truckers kept rolling in Broadway tripper work until 1935. The 120-class, which had seen duty on all lines as trippers in later years, was finally taken out of all service in the summer of 1936 and reached the scrap pile in 1939.

VALPARAISO LINE, 1917-1938:

After the Gary & Valparaiso Railway took over the Valpo operation in 1917, cars operated directly to and from North Broadway loop. Two large steel "submarine" cars, numbers 50 and 51, were used. They had bodies duplicating the cars used on the International Railway Company Buffalo-Niagara Falls high-speed line, but the motor equipment of the Gary units was not for fast operation. Additional trippers between Valparaiso and the lakes were run in season as required, using rented Gary cars 105 and 107 or others.

In November, 1924, the two 55,000 lb. two-man cars were replaced by two 42,500 lb. low-floor safety-type one-man cars. The same hourly service and running time were maintained. During the first ten months of operation the cost of conducting transportation was reduced by 29.7%. Despite a reduction of $1800 a month in revenue from the transportation of milk, which could not be handled on the new cars, and the continued diversion of traffic to highways, the year-round business improved and the cost was reduced.

These cars, numbered 1 and 2, were fitted with high back seats and had toilet compartments, which were removed in the late thirties and replaced by ordinary rattan walkover seating. A third car, number 3, was maintained as a spare in the Valpo corrugated iron barn, rotating in regular service with the other two.

For a while, an hourly schedule was run. But by the late 1920's, the headway had been lengthened to two hours thru and hourly to Garyton. The schedule was worked out so that cars made alternate round trips to Valpo and Garyton.

On October 23, 1938 the line was abandoned between Garyton and Valparaiso. Service on the remaining segment from Gary to Garyton was later doubled, daily except Sunday. Former Crown Point cars 50 and 51, reconditioned for this line, worked between North Broadway and Garyton loops until replaced by busses in 1942.

FUNERAL SERVICE:

In 1915 Calvary Cemetery was established on Gary & Interurban, near Garyton. At the request of church authorities the company put a funeral car into service, which became available to all other cemeteries on the system and saw duty on all lines of the company.

FREIGHT SERVICE:

An effort was made to develop a freight business, both local and interline with steam and electric railways. After much difficulty some interchanges were constructed to steam roads. An interchange was also made between the Air Line and the Chicago South Bend & Northern Indiana Railway at LaPorte. Six box cars were purchased and a local freight service operated between Hammond, Gary, LaPorte, South Bend and Goshen.

After the G&I merger, freight solicitation was intensified, particularly in the farming districts along the lines. The railway claimed to give an express service at freight rates and was handling LCL shipments on all interurbans east of Gary. By 1916, forty shippers were using this service.

Milk was a most important commodity. During this period, when roads were hardly more than a series of ruts, farmers had difficulties in getting milk into town and the interurban was a welcome convenience to them. Milk cars were run between LaPorte, Chesterton, Valparaiso, Gary, Hammond and Indiana Harbor. Milk traffic rose from a daily 70 cans in 1913 to 270 cans daily in 1916. With abandonment of the GSB&C in 1917 nearly all freight service ended, but a milk train continued to work between Valparaiso and Hammond until 1924.

Main freight station was in Gary, at 11th & Broadway, opposite the passenger depot. Most freights were handled by the 1001, but after 1002 was built it took over the milk trains and in turn was helped out at times by 404, which by then had been converted to a work car. After 1917, 404 usually handled the milk run pulling trailers 2300 and 2301 as needed, while 1002 became a work car and finally wound up as a sweeper in 1928. The Cloverleaf Dairy Company continued to receive a tank car of oil now and then via interurban until abandonment of the Garyton line in 1942. This company was located on 11th Avenue near Broadway and the tank car was set out on a siding right in the street. In later years, car 124 was usually given the job of switching this car from the Michigan Central interchange.

Gary & Hobart Traction had two box cars assigned to ice haulage. Ice was cut from Lake George in winter, stored at Hobart till needed and then hauled in for sale, using a single-truck work motor car as a locomotive.

Car 1 near Wahob, by B. L. Stone

Fare Structure:

In the late 1920's, fares in Gary were 8¢ with tokens priced at 14 for $1. The longer routes had two additional 6¢ or 8¢ zones, as shown on the maps, except the Valparaiso line, where a station-to-station tariff was in effect. Later years saw an increase of the street car fare to 10¢.

To offset light Sunday riding, a Sunday pass was inaugurated in the spring of 1928. This pass sold for a quarter and entitled the bearer to unlimited riding on the entire system for the date of sale, except that a charge of 10¢ was later instituted for each use on the Valparaiso or Crown Point divisions. The Sunday pass became very popular and was continued thruout the rest of the street car days.

In order to attract short haul riders in the inner area of Gary, a nickel zone fare was established in 1931 on Fifth Avenue, Eleventh Avenue and Broadway north of the Pennsylvania Railroad. Control of the zone fare was obtained by pay-leave collection outbound from town and pay-enter inbound. The rear door was so arranged that it could be placed on direct remote control from the motorman's position (to permit its use for loading outbound), closed and cut off (to prevent its use for exit after leaving the upper Broadway area outbound), or on automatic treadle operation. No transfers were issued on the 5¢ fare. Despite the limitations on its use, the nickel fare was much used and did a lot to increase revenue during the depression. Due to the rising costs of operation and denser loading, this bargain fare was discontinued during World War II.

Decline of Rail Service:

The depression hit Gary hard and with it the Gary Railways. Steel mill output was greatly reduced and National Tube shut down completely in 1932. Immediate result on Gary Railways was the end of trailer operation.

Ironically, the first interurban line to be converted to bus was the last one rehabilitated and that with the finest cars the company owned-- the Crown Point line. The last regular car ran on June 17, 1933. On Monday, March 5, 1934, after almost a year of suspension of service, a car was run over the line in a trial to demonstrate its condition, but the line was torn up in the following months.

Early in 1935 the Miller line was replaced by buses. On January 29, 1938, the last cars ran to the Tin Mill and the line was cut back to the Sheet Mill loop.

Hearings for abandonment of the Valparaiso Division east of Garyton were begun May 11, 1938. The Valpo line was probably the most scenic interurban ride in the Chicago area and a great favorite with railfans. Nevertheless, the line was losing steadily. Its losses of pre-Gary Railways days have already been mentioned, but these losses increased again with the coming of the depression, and the line was enabled to continue only thru deferred maintenance. The first three months of 1938 showed a $7000 loss and the property was in a shape that would require an expenditure of $25,000 to restore it. Altho only a few hundred patrons used the line daily, over 1500 joined in protest to its proposed abandonment. The commission finally conceded the loss was excessive and granted permission for abandonment, which took place at the close of business October 22, 1938.

Conversion of the Indiana Harbor and Hobart lines to bus was effected on March 19, 1939, and altho regular car service had ceased the preceding day, Col. Hamilton, operating head of Gary Railways, arranged for a final inspection trip by CERA on the 19th.

It was at this time that the Indiana Harbor line was shortened to the Pennsy crossing on Fifth Avenue, with branch service on Bridge and Buchanan Streets. These latter two lines were converted to bus late in 1940, while car service on Fifth came to an end in January 1941. Garyton was the next replacement, trolleys running for the last time on January 25, 1942.

At the request of the Office of Defense Transportation the bus conversion program was brought to a halt for the duration of the war, and the three remaining car lines, Hammond, Tube Works and Broadway, went to work to handle Gary's greatest loads ever. Annual passengers carried rose from the 1932 low of 7 million to 14 million in 1940, 21 million in 1942, 31 million in 1943, and 33 million in 1944. Thereafter the volume gradually declined. The majority of the wartime load moved on Broadway and the 41 cars remaining again more than proved their worth.

In compliance with Securities Exchange Commission rulings, Gary Railways was sold in 1942 to a new company, the Gary Railways, Inc.

With the end of the war and the relaxation of new equipment and gasoline restrictions, the conversion program was resumed. The Hammond line was changed over on August 21, 1946. Ten days later the Broadway line went to bus, and altho the Tube Works line was still operating by rail, due to insufficient buses, the farewell celebrations were held. Seven cars filled with representatives of civic groups, business men and city officials participated in the event. The return trip was made in some of the new buses.

For its remaining days, ten cars were moved to a siding near the Tube Works, where they could be used to service the line. Only two were required to move the mill workers to Fifth and Broadway, but the others were standby for repairs on the now shop-less line. Finally, on February 28, 1947 the last street cars ran, bringing to a close the street railway history of Gary.

THE THREE TYPES OF AIR LINE PASSENGER CARS:
1 - #102 was one of the two original cars in 1907, famous for painted destinations ''New York'' and
    ''Chicago''.
2 - Two years later, three trailers were added--certainly austere cars by comparison.
3 - In 1912, motor cars 103-104 arrived and the trailers were renumbered to make way (see roster).

Pages 20 through 31 present a pictorial album, arranged approximately in chronological sequence, showing many types of Gary's city, suburban and service cars.

Here also is a roster of cars listing the characteristics of all rolling stock used on the system. Created by James J. Buckley and Leonard Foitl for CERA's "Electric Railways of Indiana" in 1960, it consolidated the information from all previously published sources, with additions and corrections. The state of research has continued to progress so that it is possible to include further improvements in this Enlarged Edition of "Gary Railways".

GARY LINES

(UNDERLYING PROPERTIES)

CAR NUMBER	BUILDER	BUILT	TRUCKS	MOTORS	CONTROL	WEIGHT	SEATS	LENGTH OVERALL	WIDTH OVERALL	HEIGHT OVER ROOF	RETIRED	REMARKS
GOSHEN SOUTH BEND & CHICAGO RAILROAD:												
101-102	Niles	'07	Baldwin MCB	4-WH			50	49'-6"				Combination cars, to Gary & Int RR 400-401 in 1913.
103-104	McG-Cummings	'12	McG. 70A	4-GE73	M	70,000	60	56'-0"	9'-6"	13'-6"	'39	Combination cars, "Ohm" and "Ampere" resp. To Gary & Int RR 402-403 1913.
105-107	McG-Cummings	'09	McG. 10A	Trail	None		48	44'-0"	8'-4"	11'-6"	'26	Originally 103-105, to Gary & Int RR 500,2300 and 2301 in 1913.
1001	McG-Cummings	'12	McG. 70A	4-GE285		46,000	—	50'-0"	8'-9"	12'-0"	'51	Express motor, to G&I RR 1001 in 1913
2000-2002			Arch Bar	Trail	None		—	41'-0"				Box cars, purchased second hand in 1912. To G&I RR in 1913.
2003-2005	McG-Cummings	'12	Arch Bar	Trail	None		—				'23	Box cars, to G&I RR 2003-2005 in 1913
3000	McG-Cummings	'12	McGuire	4-WH		62,000	—					Work motor, to G&I RR 3000 in 1913.
GARY & SOUTHERN TRACTION COMPANY:												
2,4	Niles	'12	Baldwin 73-18-K	4-WH307	K35G	46,000	44	44'-6"	8'-8"	11'-5"		Passenger interurbans, 4 burned at Goodrum in 1919.
6,8	Niles	'12	Baldwin 73-18-K	4-WH307	K35G	46,000	44	44'-6"	8'-8"	11'-5"		Combination cars, to Gary Rys P3 and P4 in 1929.
Unknown							—					Single truck work car.
VALPARAISO & NORTHERN RAILWAY:												
20	McG-Cummings	'09	McG. 10A	4-GE			38	41'-6"	8'-8"		'26	Built as Denver & Intermountain Ry #20, To G&I RR 404 in 1913.
101-102							46	45'-0"			'23	Purchased second hand 1910. To G&I RR 1913, one rebuilt to line car 100 and the other to funeral car CALVARY.
GARY & VALPARAISO RAILWAY:												
1-2	Kuhlman	'24	Brill 77E1	4-GE-247	K35JJ	42,480	44	44'-8"	8'-6"	11'-0"	'47	To Gary Railways 1-2 in 1925.
50-51	Kuhlman	'18	Taylor	4-GE-203P	K35G2	56,940	65	54'-7"	8'-6"	11'-6"	'39	To Gary Railways P1-P2 in 1928.
100							—	45'-0"			'23	Line car, acquired 1917 from G&I RR. Wrecked at Wahob Sept.1923.
404	McG-Cummings	'09	McG. 10A	4-GE80	K35G2			41'-6"	8'-8"		'26	Acquired 1917 from G&I RR, made into work car.
1501-1502			Arch Bar	Trail	None		—	41'-0"			'26	Box cars, acquired 1917 from G&I RR.
2300-2301	McG-Cummings	'09	McG. 10A	Trail	None		—	44'-0"	8'-6"	11'-6"	'23	Milk cars, acquired 1917 from G&I RR.
CALVARY							—	45'-0"			'23	Funeral car, from G&I RR in 1917.
EAST CHICAGO STREET RAILWAY:												
125-128	McG-Cummings	'13	McG. 10A	4-GE80	K28	44,000	44	44'-0"	8'-9"	11'-10"	'40	Leased to the G&I RR from 1913 to 1917. Sold 1917 to Gary Street Ry.
GARY HOBART & EASTERN TRACTION COMPANY **GARY & HOBART TRACTION COMPANY:**												
1	Wason-General Elec.	'09	Wason	2-GE72A		72,000	44	50'-0"	9'-6"	11'-7"		Gas electric car, originally GE 3, used in 1912 on GH&E as a demonstrator, lettered GH&E 1. Sold 1914 by GE to Luce Electric Line 300.
1	Pullman	'95	CCRy. Moore	2-WH12A		20,000	25	30'-0"	7'-7"	10'-11"	'23	Work car. Purchased 1914 from Chicago City Ry. 2316, originally number 1916.
2	St Louis	'08	St.L. 47B	4-WH101A	K28	36,000	40	41'-0"	8'-4"	11'-6"	'27	Originally Springfield (Ill.) & Clear Lake 3 or 4, purchased 1914 from St. Louis. Renumbered 5 in 1920.
3	St Louis	'08	St.L. 47B	4-WH101A	K28	36,000	40	41'-0"	8'-4"	11'-6"	'26	Same origin as above. To Gary Rys. 25 in 1925.
3-5	Kuhlman	'25	Brill 77E1	4-GE247I	K35PP	42,520	44	44'-8"	8'-8"	11'-0"	'47	To Gary Railways 3-5 in 1925.
5	St Louis	'08	St.L. 47B	4-WH101A	K28	36,000	40	41'-0"	8'-4"	11'-6"	'27	Former number 2, sold to Gary Rys.26 in 1925.
7	Niles		Peckham 9	4-WH532A	K35G2			47'-0"			'26	Acquired second hand in 1916, to Gary Railways 27 in 1925.
10	St Louis	'20	St.L. 7	2-GE		16,000	32	28'-0"	8'-0"	10'-2"		Birney, sold 1923 to Benton Harbor-St.Joe Ry. & Light Co.
Unknown											'15	Two single-truck open cars, purchased second hand in 1914.

B&LE - Buffalo & Lake Erie Traction Co.
CSL - Chicago Surface Lines
CUT - Chicago Union Traction Co.

DM&CI - Des Moines & Central Iowa Railroad
G&I RR - Gary & Interurban Railroad
GSB&C - Goshen South Bend & Chicago Railroad

G&ST - Gary & Southern Traction Co.
G&V - Gary & Valparaiso Railway
V&N - Valparaiso & Northern Railway

GARY LINES

(Including GARY & INTERURBAN RY. and GARY RAILWAYS)

CAR NUMBER	BUILDER	BUILT	TRUCKS	MOTORS	CONTROL	WEIGHT	SEATS	LENGTH OVERALL	WIDTH OVERALL	HEIGHT OVER ROOF	RETIRED	REMARKS
CITY AND SUBURBAN CARS												
1-2	Kuhlman	'24	Brill 77E1	4-GE247	K35JJ	42,480	46	44'-8"	8'-6"	11'-0"	'47	Ex-Gary & Valparaiso Ry, acquired 1925. Originally had 44 seats.
3-5	Kuhlman	'25	Brill 77E1	4-GE247I	K35PP	42,520	46	44'-8"	8'-8"	11'-0"	'47	Ex-Gary & Hobart Traction Co, acquired 1925. Originally had 44 seats.
6-10	Cummings	'26	Cumm'gs 62	4-GE265	K35JJ	37,000	46	44'-8"	8'-8"	10'-9"	'46	No. 9 wrecked 4-28-27 in collision with 201 on Fifth Avenue.
9	Cummings	'27	Cumm'gs 62	4-GE247	K35PP	40,000	46	44'-8"	8'-8"	10'-9"	'46	Replaced first #9
11-17	Cummings	'26	Cumm'gs 62	4-GE247	K35PP	37,000	46	44'-8"	8'-8"	10'-9"	'46	
18	Cummings	'27	Cumm'gs 62	4-GE247	K35PP	40,000	46	44'-8"	8'-8"	10'-9"	'46	
19-27	Cummings	'27	Cumm'gs 62	4-GE265	K75A	37,000	52	44'-0"	8'-8"	11'-0"	'46	
25-26	St.Louis	'08	St.L 47B	4-WH101A	K28	36,000	40	41'-0"	8'-4"	11'-6"	'26	Ex-Gary & Hobart Traction Co, acquired 1925. No. 26 retired in 1927.
27	Niles		Peckham 9	4-WH532A	K35C2			47'-0"			'26	Ex-Gary & Hobart Traction Co, acquired 1925.
50-51	Cummings	'29	Cumm'gs 64	4-GE247	K75F	42,000	50	44'-10"	9'-0"	10'-9"	'46	Single end cars originally used in Crown Point service.
100								45'-0"			'23	Acquired 1913 from Valparaiso & Northern Ry, made line car in 1914, to Gary & Valparaiso Ry 12-3-17.
101	Danville	'08	Brill 27G1	4-GE80	K28B	40,000	44	42'-0"	8'-4"	12'-0"	'37	Used only for exhibition purposes after 1927.
102-104	Danville	'08	Brill 27G1	2-GE80	K10	38,000	44	42'-0"	8'-4"	12'-0"	'27	
105	McG-Cummings	'09	McG. 10A	4-GE80	K28B	46,000	46	44'-0"	9'-0"	11'-6"	'29	Rebuilt to work car 1923, to plow P3 1927.
106	McG-Cummings	'09	McG. 10A	4-GE80	K28B	46,000	46	44'-0"	9'-0"	11'-6"	'37	Rebuilt to express car 1002 in 1914.
107	McG-Cummings	'09	McG. 10A	4-GE80	K28B	46,000	46	44'-0"	9'-0"	11'-6"	'37	Rebuilt to work car 1923, to plow P4 1927.
108	McG-Cummings	'09	McG. 10A	4-GE80	K28B	46,000	46	44'-0"	9'-0"	11'-6"	'46	Renumbered 106 in 1914 and rebuilt to sweeper S6 in 1928.
109	McG-Cummings	'10	McG. 10A	4-GE203F	K35JJ	51,000	44	44'-0"	8'-9"	12'-0"	'39	Made 1-man 1927.
110-111	McG-Cummings	'10	McG. 10A	4-GE80	K28B	46,000	44	44'-0"	8'-9"	12'-0"	'37	Made 1-man 1927.
112	McG-Cummings	'10	McG. 10A	4-GE80	K28B	46,000	44	44'-0"	8'-9"	12'-0"	'26	
113	McG-Cummings	'11	McG. 10A	4-GE203P	K35C2	51,000	40	44'-0"	8'-4"	11'-7"	'37	Made 1-man 1927.
114	McG-Cummings	'11	McG. 10A	4-GE80	K28B	46,000	40	44'-0"	8'-4"	11'-7"	'46	Rebuilt into sweeper S7 in 1928.
115	McG-Cummings	'11	McG. 10A	4-GE80	K28B	46,000	40	44'-0"	8'-4"	11'-7"	'26	
116-117	McG-Cummings	'11	McG. 10A	4-GE80	K28B	46,000	40	44'-0"	8'-4"	11'-7"	'37	Made 1-man 1927
118	McG-Cummings	'11	McG. 10A	4-GE80	K28B	46,000	40	44'-0"	8'-4"	11'-7"	'46	Rebuilt into sweeper S8 in 1928.
119	McG-Cummings	'11	McG. 10A	4-GE80	K28B	46,000	40	44'-0"	8'-4"	11'-7"	'46	Rebuilt into line car L1 in 1927.
120	McG-Cummings	'11	McG. 10A	4-GE226	K35G	44,000	44	44'-0"	8'-9"	11'-10"	'40	Rebuilt with arch roof 1922
121-124	McG-Cummings	'13	McG. 10A	4-GE226	K35C2	44,000	44	44'-0"	8'-9"	11'-10"	'40	Rebuilt with arch roof 1922, 124 to sand car in 1940 and retired 1946.
125-128	McG-Cummings	'13	McG. 10A	4-GE226	K35C2	44,000	44	44'-0"	8'-9"	11'-10"	'40	From East Chicago St. Ry. in 1917. Rebuilt 1922 with arch roofs.
201-202	McG-Cummings	'18	McG. 46	4-WH514A	HLD	43,000	56	45'-0"	8'-6"	11'-0"		201 wrecked 4-28-27. 202 retired 1937
203-212	Kuhlman	'19	Brill 77E1	4-GE247	K35JJ	37,000	52	48'-1"	8'-4"	10'-11"	See below	Peter Witts, rebuilt 1927 by Cummings to one-man. Center doors replaced by rear doors. Originally had 4-GE258 motors, K12 control, 51 seats.
213-218	Kuhlman	'19	Brill 77E1	4-GE247	K35C2	37,000	52	48'-1"	8'-4"	10'-11"	See below	Peter Witts, rebuilt 1927 by Cummings. Acquired 1923 from U.S. Government, were operated by Buffalo & Lake Erie Traction Co. as 231-236.
301-304	McG-Cummings	'18	McGuire	Trail	None	30,175	52	47'-0"	8'-6"	11'-0"	'37	
305-309	Kuhlman	'19	Brill 67F	Trail	None	32,000	58	50'-0"	8'-6"	11'-0"	'37	
310-313	Kuhlman	'19	Brill 67F	Trail	None	32,000	52	50'-0"	8'-6"	11'-0"	'37	Acquired 1923 from U. S. Government, were operated by B&LE as 266-269.
400-401	Niles	'07	Baldwin MCB	4-WH			50	49'-6"				Acquired 1913 from GSB&C RR. 400 wrecked 1-1-16, 401 body to Milwaukee Northern 51, trucks and motors to 3000.
402-403	McG-Cummings	'12	McG. 70A	4-GE73	M	70,000	60	56'-0"	9'-6"	13'-6"	'39	From GSB&C 1913, sold 1917 to Inter-Urban Ry, became DM&CI 1708-1709.
404	McG-Cummings	'09	McG. 10A	4-GE	K35C2		38	41'-6"	8'-8"		'26	From V&N 1913, to Gary & Valparaiso Ry 12-3-17.
500	McG-Cummings	'09	McG. 10A	Trail	None		48	44'-0"	8'-6"	11'-6"	'26	From GSB&C RR 1913.
601	Chicago Union Traction Co	'00	Curtis OHM	4-GE52	K12	42,300	36	39'-6"	7'-9"	11'-3"	'26	Orig CUT, acquired 1916 from CSL 1456. Became 601 6-5-18.
602	Chicago Union Traction Co	'00	Curtis OHM	4-GE52	K12	42,300	36	39'-6"	7'-9"	11'-3"	'26	Orig CUT, acquired 1916 from CSL 1429. Became 602 10-15-20.
603	Chicago Union Traction Co	'00	Curtis OHM	4-GE52	K12	42,300	36	39'-6"	7'-9"	11'-3"	'27	Orig CUT, acquired 1916 from CSL 1479. Became 603 11-1-20.
604	Chicago Union Traction Co	'00	Curtis OHM	4-GE52	K28	42,300	36	39'-6"	7'-9"	11'-3"	'27	Orig CUT, acquired 1917 from CSL 1485. Became 604 12-30-20.
701-710	American	'18	Brill 78M1B	2-GE258	K63B	16,000	32	27'-9"	8'-0"	10'-2"	'37	Birneys
711-715	McG-Cummings	'23	McG. 90	2-GE258	K63G	17,000	32	30'-2"	8'-0"	10'-2"	'37	Double door Birneys
716-720	Cummings	'25	Cumm'gs 90	2-GE264	C90	17,000	32	30'-2"	8'-0"	10'-2"	'37	Double door Birneys

Retirement dates of cars 203-218:
#203-207, 1946; #208-211, 1940; #212-213, 1947; #214, 1946; #215-217, 1947; #218, 1946.

GARY LINES

(Including GARY & INTERURBAN RY. and GARY RAILWAYS), continued.

CAR NUMBER	BUILDER	BUILT	TRUCKS	MOTORS	CONTROL	WEIGHT	SEATS	LENGTH OVERALL	WIDTH OVERALL	HEIGHT OVER ROOF	RETIRED	REMARKS
FREIGHT AND SERVICE CARS												
1001	McG-Cummings	'12	McG. 70A	4-GE285		46,000	—	50'-0"	8'-9"	12'-0"	'51	Express motor from GSB&C RR 1913. Sold 1917 to Inter-Urban Ry, later became DM&CI 1600.
1002	McG-Cummings	'09	McG. 10A	4-GE80	K35PP	46,000	—	44'-0"	9'-0"	11'-6"	'37	Rebuilt from 106 in 1914, became sweeper S5 in 1928.
1500	Gary St. Rwy.	'19	Baldwin 73-18	4-WH307	K35G		—	48'-0"			'34	Work motor rebuilt from G&ST 4.
1501			Arch Bar	Trail	None		—	41'-0"			'26	Box car orig 2002. To G&V 1917.
1502			Arch Bar	Trail	None		—				'26	Box car, acquired from Barnes Ice & Coal Co. To G&V 1917.
2000			Arch Bar	Trail	None		—	41'-0"			'38	Box car, Ex-GSB&C RR 2000. Became 2001 in 1922.
2001				Trail	None		—					Portable substation, sold to Calumet Electric Company.
2001			Arch Bar	Trail	None		—	41'-0"			'38	Box car, Ex-2000.
2002			Arch Bar	Trail	None		—	41'-0"			'26	Box car, renumbered 1501
2002	McG-Cummings	'12	Arch Bar	Trail	None		—					Flat car, Ex-2003.
2003	McG-Cummings	'12	Arch Bar	Trail	None		—					Box car, made flat car 2002 5-15-22.
2004-2005	McG-Cummings	'12	Arch Bar	Trail	None		—				'23	Box cars, Ex-GSB&C RR, acquired 1913 Scrapped 1923.
2300-2301	McG-Cummings	'09	McG. 10A	Trail	None		—	44'-0"	8'-6"	11'-6"	'23	Milk cars, Ex-GSB&C RR passenger trailers, to G&V Ry in 1917.
3000	McG-Cummings	'12	Baldwin MCB	4-WH		62,000	—					Sold, purchaser unknown. Double truck work motor.
CALVARY								45'-0"			'23	Funeral car, rebuilt 1915 from V&N pass car. To G&V Ry 1917
L1	Gary Rys Co	'27	McG. 10A	4-GE80	K35PP	46,000	—	44'-0"	8'-9"	12'-0"	'46	Line car, rebuilt from pass car 119.
P1	McG-Cummings	'08	McG. 8DL	2-GE80	K10	30,000	—				'25	Single truck plow, retired 1925.
P1-P2	Gary Rys Co	'28	Taylor	4-GE203P	K35PP	58,000	—	63'-0"	8'-6"	11'-6"	'39	DT plows, rebuilt from G&V Ry 50-51.
P3-P4	Gary Rys Co	'27	McG. 10A	4-GE80	K28B	48,000	—	53'-6"	9'-0"	11'-6"	'29	DT plows, rebuilt from work cars 105 and 107.
P3-P4	Gary Rys Co	'29	Baldwin 73-18-K	4-WH307	K35G	48,000	—	54'-0"	8'-8"	11'-5"		DT plows, rebuilt from G&ST 6 and 8. P3 retired 1942, P4 retired 1939.
S2	McG-Cummings	'10	McGuire	4-GE80	K10	30,000	—	28'-3"	7'-2"	10'-9"	'46	ST sweeper,
S3	McG-Cummings	'13	McGuire	4-GE90	K10	30,000	—	28'-3"	7'-2"	10'-9"	'46	ST sweeper,
S4	McG-Cummings	'25	McGuire	4-GE80	K10	30,000	—	28'-3"	7'-2"	10'-9"	'46	ST sweeper,
S5	Gary Rys Co	'28	McG. 10A	4-GE80	K35PP	47,000	—	58'-1"	9'-0"	11'-6"	'37	Double truck sweeper, rebuilt from 1002.
S6-S8	Gary Rys Co	'28	McG. 10A	4-GE80	K35PP	47,000	—	58'-1"	9'-0"	11'-6"	'46	DT sweepers, rebuilt from 106,114 and 118 resp.

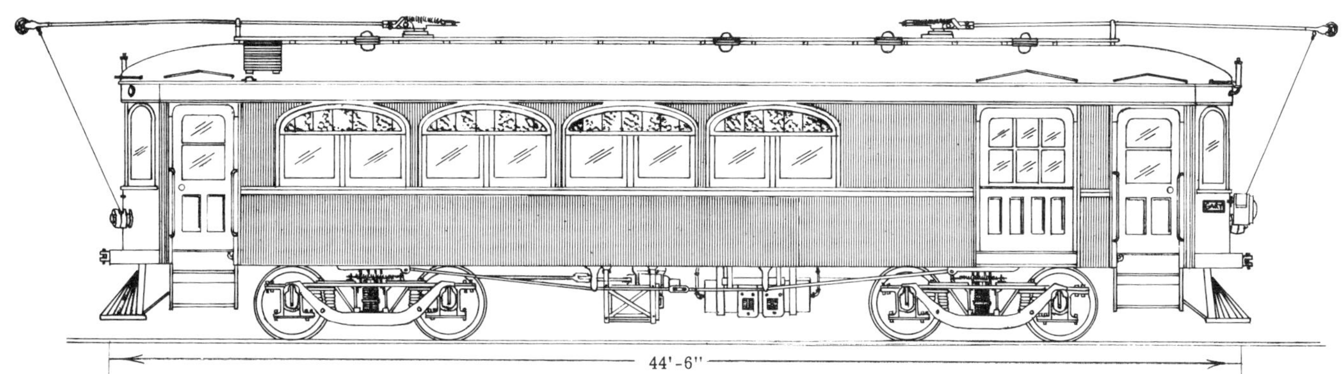

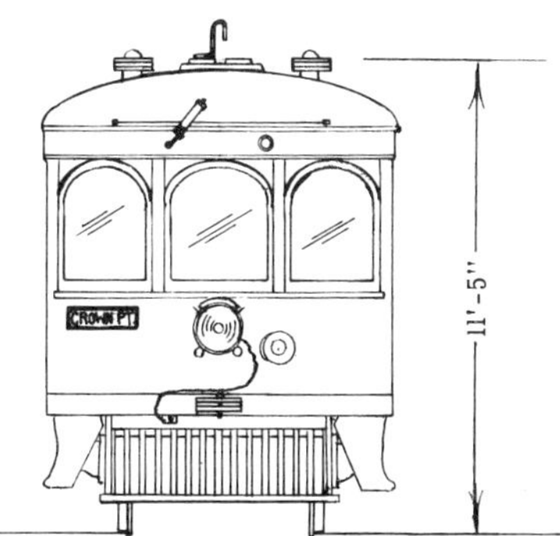

Combines #6 and #8, along with two coaches, all built by Niles in 1912, comprised Gary & Southern Traction's entire passenger roster. Recognizing the industrial nature of the traffic, the road specified rattan seating, plainer than one would predict from the exterior style of the car. But the folding wooden slat seats in the baggage compartments would have been familiar to patrons of many an interurban line. Car interiors were quartered oak with a dark weathered finish. The combines later served as snowplows, hurriedly converted early in 1929 when the weather pinpointed the property's snow-fighting apparatus as a weak spot.

(Drawing by Leonard Foitl)

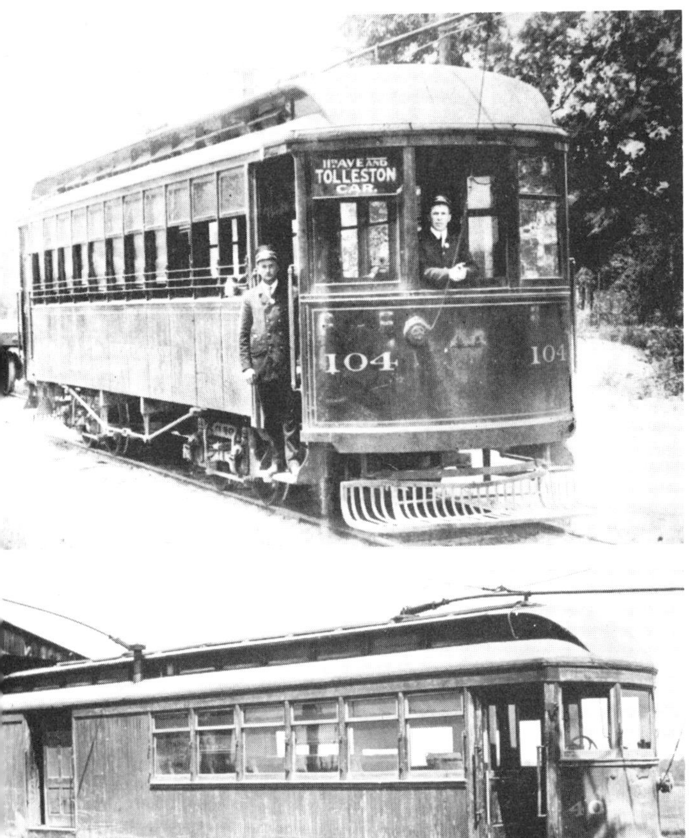

SOME OF THE OLDER CARS:
Having its inception as late as it did, the system concentrated on closed-body cars--double-truckers right from the start. The only four-wheelers were Birneys.

1-Car 108 on Broadway, Gary, signed for the Hammond run. Behind the fence at the left, cars of the "South Shore Lines" are visible. (Ed Frank collection)

2-#109 marked "Tolleston Chase" for a short-turn on the Hammond line. (James J. Buckley)

3-At Gary barn, #121 models its new arch roof.

4-Also with a rebuilt roof, #126 works Broadway. (Two photos, Bortz Studios)

5-#104 at the Pennsy crossing on 11th Avenue for the opening of the Tolleston line, 1910.

6-#404 after its best days were over. (Bortz Studios)

7-At North Broadway in 1919 or 1920, an assortment of cars typical of the period: #101, one of the system's original city cars; #710, a new Birney; and #1485, an old Chicago castoff.

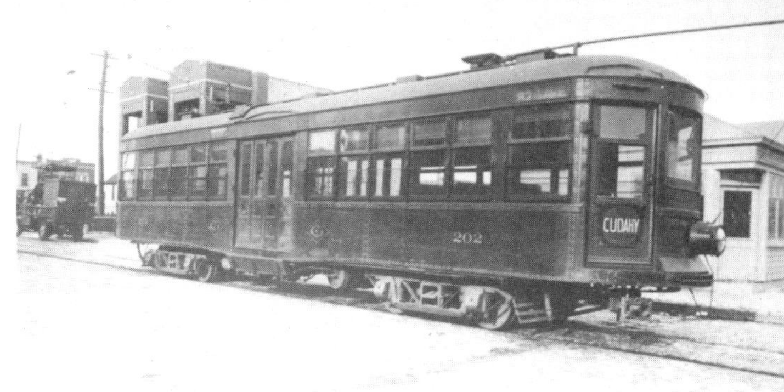

NEW CARS OF 1918-19:

With the Birneys came a brief flirtation with center-door trains. Above right: Motor #202 on Indiana Harbor division. Above: Trailer #303 at Gary barns. Soon Gary chose Peter Witts like #209 below. Cars 203-212 were built for Gary on Kuhlman order 681; almost identical #213-218 came later from a New York interurban line. More center-door trailers were acquired with each group. (Three photos, Bortz Studios)

Within a decade the Peter Witts were misfits in a fleet of front-entrance, rear-treadle-exit one-man cars. So they went to Cummings for a thoro rebuilding. In this form, some of them ran for another twenty years. At right: #207 westbound on 2nd Avenue in 1938 (Robert V. Mehlenbeck). Below right: #204 at Coke Plant station, Tube Works line (John F. Humiston). At bottom: #205 readying for departure from North Broadway for 45th Avenue, July 25, 1937 (R. V. Mehlenbeck).

CARS 6-18:
(Across the bottom of these two pages)

Ordered in March 1926 and delivered in July were five more cars (#6-10), similar to #1-5 but with quite different proportions of window area. For these cars and all subsequent ones, Gary Railways turned to Cummings Car & Coach Company at Paris, Illinois. As there was no smoker, high-backed green plush seats were used thruout. Initially the cars were assigned, three to Indiana Harbor and two to Hobart. At right, on May 15, 1937, #8 is about to cross the South Shore Line at Cline Avenue on the Indiana Harbor run (Malcolm D. McCarter collection).

Then in June 1926, seven more cars (#11-17) were ordered for the Hammond line, where they entered service the next January. Tho almost identical to the previous order, these had 40-HP motors (instead of 35 HP), different control, and could be distinguished by details, such as sliding doors, anticlimbers and a green (rather than gray) linoleum floor. Far right: #16 in Hammond on Hammond Division run 5 (William C. Janssen).

Car 18 was ordered in January 1927, also for the Hammond line. Finally a second #9 was ordered for Indiana Harbor, replacing the first one which was destroyed in April. Both of these cars were equipped like #11-17.

CARS 711-720:

In the 1920's ten double-door Birneys (#711-720) were added. At right: The first of them. This dark color scheme was soon changed to traction orange with a brownish red roof. Doors and window sash were dark maroon; underbody, dark red. Headlights, retrievers, anticlimbers and in the final years all the lettering and striping were black, except the GRys emblem which was gold, outlined in red.... Opposite page: The yard across from the Gary car barn, loaded with seven Birneys, November 21, 1927. Both single- and double- door cars are visible (George Krambles collection).

CARS 1-5:

Gary next turned to a more luxurious design. Cars 1-2, on Kuhlman order 823, came in 1924 lettered for the Valparaiso interurban line; 3-5 on order 851 followed the next year with the Hobart company's name. However, assignments were later adjusted and all cars later appeared in ordinary city service, ending their careers on the very last line, Tube Works. In the mid-1930's, the high-back seats, upholstered in leather in the smokers and mohair plush elsewhere, were changed to more austere low rattan seats and the lavatories were removed, but the cars remained partitioned into smoker and coach sections.

Opposite page: Builder's photo of car 1 (George Krambles collection)...Above left: Car 5 at North Broadway for Hobart trip, July 25, 1937 (Robert V. Mehlenbeck)...Below left: Car 4 at Broadway and 7th later on (Robert W. Gibson)...Below: Plan showing original arrangement (Brill Magazine).

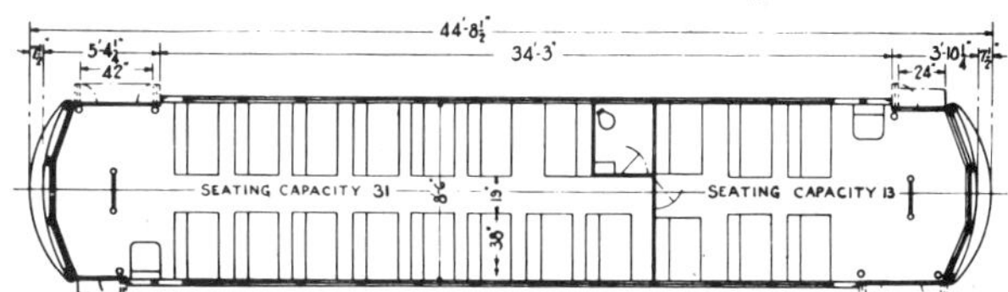

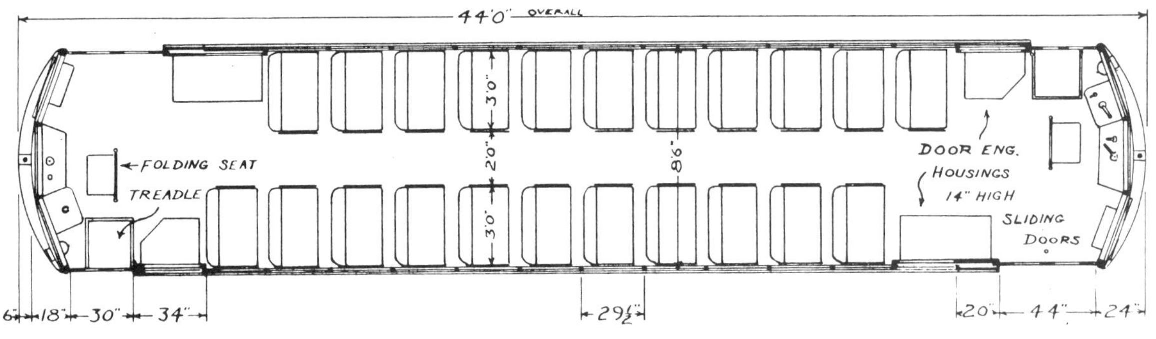

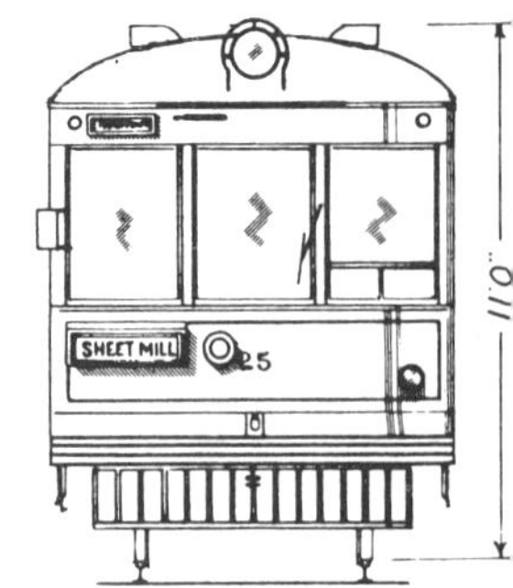

Truck centers--21 ft. 6 in.   Truck wheelbase--5 ft. 4 in.   Wheel diameter--26 in.

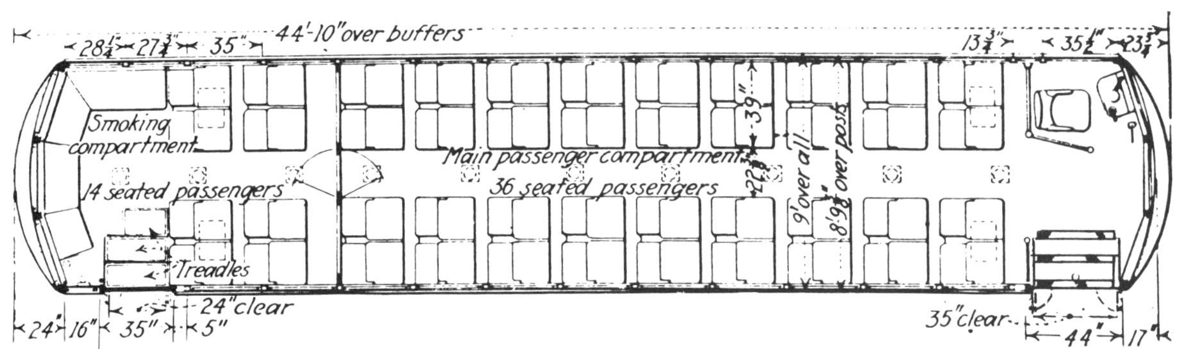

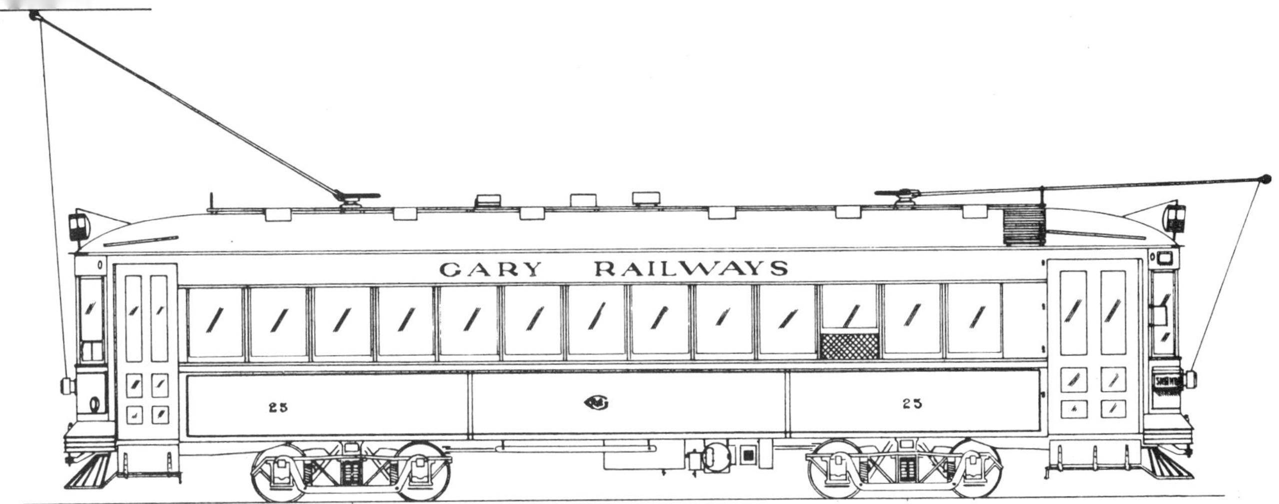

CARS 19-27:
Ordered at the same time as #18 were nine city cars further refining the clean styling of the previous groups. The low dash was of special note. Semi-individual seats were upholstered in brown genuine Spanish leather. For local service only 35-HP motors were required. A fixed pilot was applied rather than the fender arrangement seen on city cars elsewhere. These cars were delivered and placed in service in June 1927. Car 19 was painted over in white in 1928 and carried various advertising messages around the system for a few years.

Two cars are seen at North Broadway loop on Broadway thru-line runs to 45th Avenue, a frequent assignment for the group. Far left: #21, July 25, 1937 (Robert V. Mehlenbeck). Immediately left: #22, May 1, 1938 (Malcolm D. McCarter collection). Above: Plan and elevations were drawn by Robert W. Gibson for CERA Bulletin 84.

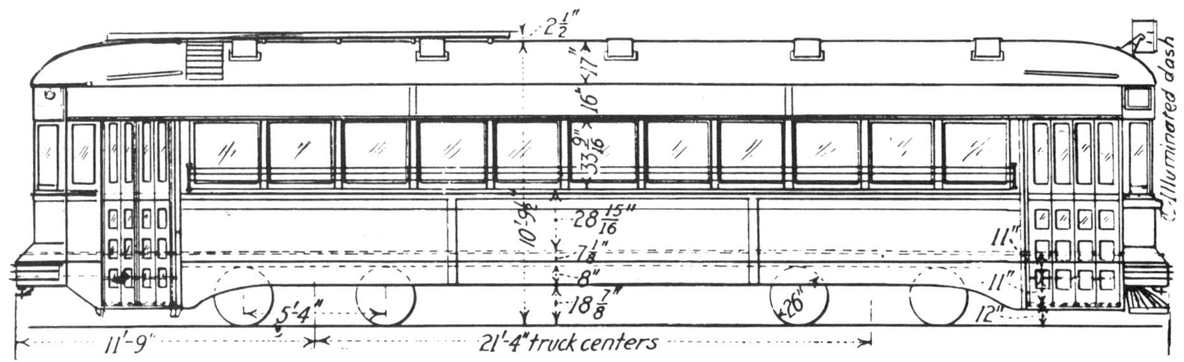

CARS 50-51: Only single-end cars in later years were bought in 1929 for the Crown Point line. After it was discontinued, the cars worked trippers between loop terminals. At right: #51 in 1935 after such a run (M. D. McCarter collection). In 1938 the Valparaiso line was cut back to a new loop at Garyton, giving the low-mileage 50's full-time work. At left: #51 at 11th & Broadway in this service (George Krambles). Drawing above appeared in Electric Railway Journal when the cars were being built.

OTHER FREIGHT AND SERVICE CARS:

Left: Air Line freight motor 1001 was built new for its job, not remade from some other unit as with so many interurban boxcars. Thus it was good enough to go to an Iowa line (which had an ownership link with the Gary system) and eventually became the last surviving Gary car, serving until the 1950's.

Right: Novel line car L.1 was rebuilt from passenger car 119 in 1927. Like the lineup of sweepers at the top of the page, the view was made in a pictorial equipment survey on November 21 of that year. (G. Krambles collection)

Opposite page, top: #105. Center: #S6, S7 or S8 in the 1930's, and #1500 at 11th & Broadway after a winter cleanup job (both, James J. Buckley collection). Above: The three conventional sweepers with #4 (#S4 on paper) in the lead (George Krambles collection). At right: #S8 at the Gary car-barns in 1938 (Ed Frank).

145TH ST.
See Map 4
Cline
Cudahy
End of 16¢ fare zone
CLINE AVENUE
Randolph End of 8¢ fare zone
Grand Calumet River
Mandell
Colfax
Elgin, Joliet & Eastern Ry. Co.
Tin Mill
Kirk Yard
Sheet Mill
North Broadway Loop See Map 3
Main Gate, U.S. Steel
Pennsylvania R.R.
Wabash R.R. Co.
BRIDGE ST.
FIFTH AVENUE
GRANT ST.
Pennsylvania Station
CHICAGO ST.
GRANT ST.
Gary
(now 9TH AV.)
MARTHA ST. (now 10TH AV.)
VIRGINIA ST.
VERMONT ST.
P.S. Bldg.
Lake Michigan
Tube Works
Coke Plant
2ND (now MASON) AVENUE
New York Central
Baltimore & Ohio
Blankville
LAKE STREET
R.R. Co.
Indiana Harbor Belt R.R.
System
7TH AV.
Miller
Indiana Harbor Belt R.R.
9TH AVENUE
Ivanhoe
Substation #2
See Map 4
West Gary
Clark Road
CLARK RD.
11TH AVENUE
End of 8¢ fare zone
Double track installed 1926 between Rutledge and Broadway
Chicago Avenue
CHASE STREET
Tolleston
RUTLEDGE ST. (now TAFT) ST.
1ST
4TH (now GARFIELD)
22ND AVENUE
Barn
23RD
Substation #1
BUCHANAN ST.
JEFFERSON ST.
BROADWAY AV.
Cloverleaf Dairy Co.
26TH AV.
Loop installed 1926, replacing a wye
CENTRAL AVENUE
Michigan Central R.R.
Kimmel
Pine St.
Aetna
Substation #4
Substation
Burns Ditch
M.C. Crossing
See Map 2
East Gary
FAIRVIEW AVENUE
East Gary
New Chicago
River
Deep
Little
Calumet River
Wabash Railroad Co.
See Map 4
Elgin, Joliet & Eastern Ry. Co.
Griffith
Michigan Central Railroad
Cleveland Street
End of 8¢ fare zone
Substation #3
37TH AVENUE
40TH AVENUE
Oak Hill Cemetery
45TH AVENUE
GRANT ST.
FILLMORE ST.
Milk Station
New York, Chicago & St. Louis R.R. Co.
Froebel
New Chicago
End of 14¢ fare zone
Pennsylvania Railroad
PENNSYLVANIA
WASHINGTON ST.
3RD ST.
Ice House
Lake George
Barn
Hobart
MAIN STREET
Elgin, Joliet & Eastern Railway Co.
Grand Trunk Ry. System
Barn
Lottaville
Chesapeake & Ohio Ry. Co.
Erie Railroad
Pennsylvania Railroad
MAIN STREET
Map scale is reduced in this area
Distance is 6 miles from Lottaville to Crown Point
Wye installed 1929
Alley south of JOLIET ST.
Crown Point
1
One Mile
ZINK
See Map 1
Michigan Central R.R.
Elgin, Joliet & Eastern Ry. Co.
Wabash R.R. Co.
Baltimore & Ohio R.R. Co.
Loop installed 1938
Lake Co.
Porter Co.
Garyton
Crisman
McCool
Babcock
Salt Creek
Pennsylvania Railroad
New York, Chicago & St. Louis R.R. Co.
Grand Trunk Ry. System
MAIN ST. (now BROADWAY
N.Y.C. System
Chesterton
5TH ST.
Goodrum Jct.
See Map 8
Esserman
Woodville Jct.
See Map 7
See Map 6
Wahob
Long Lake
Flint Lake
Burlington Beach
Valparaiso
CALUMET
Vale Park
Grand Trunk
FRANKLIN
LINCOLN
Barn installed 1927
2
One Mile

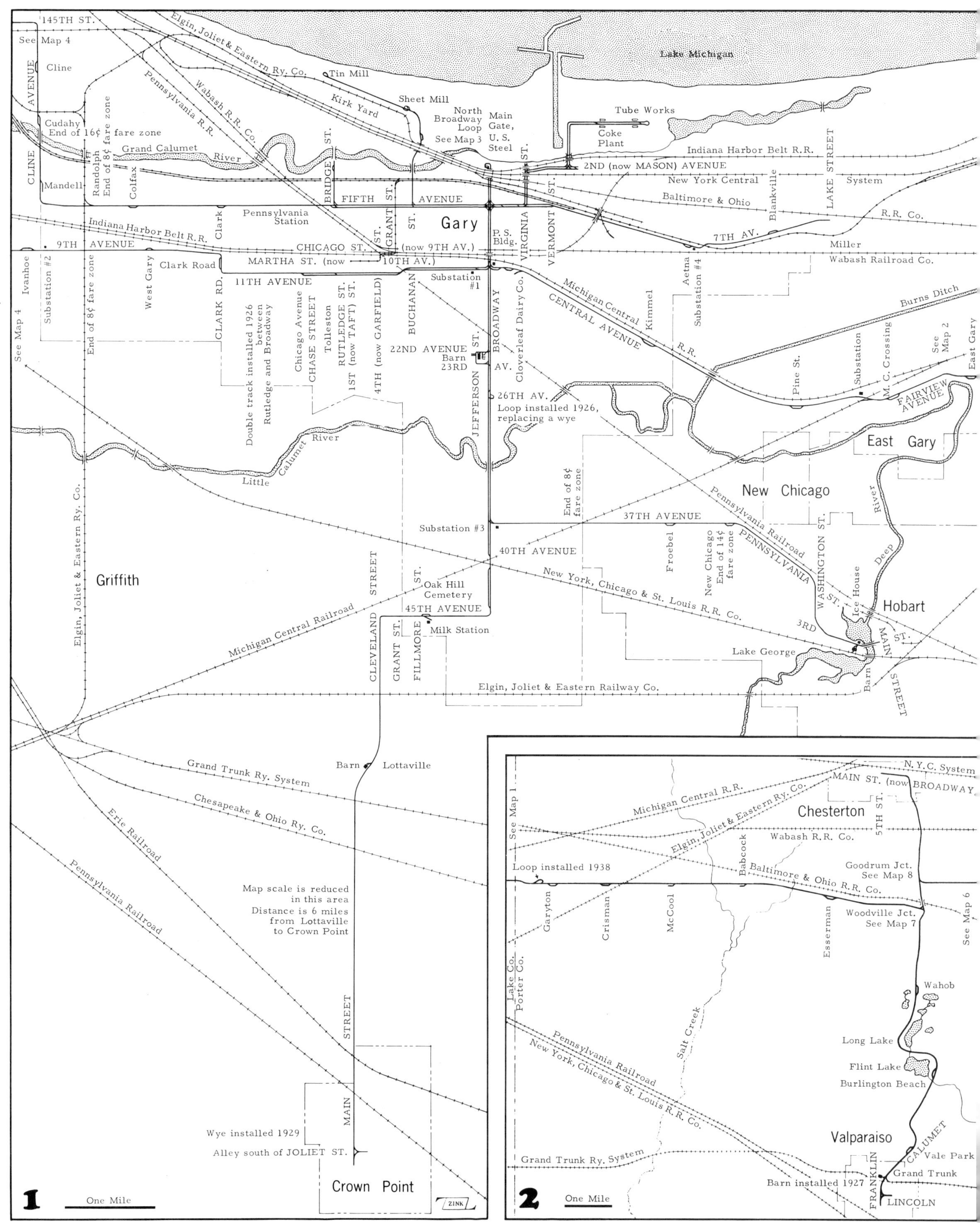

32

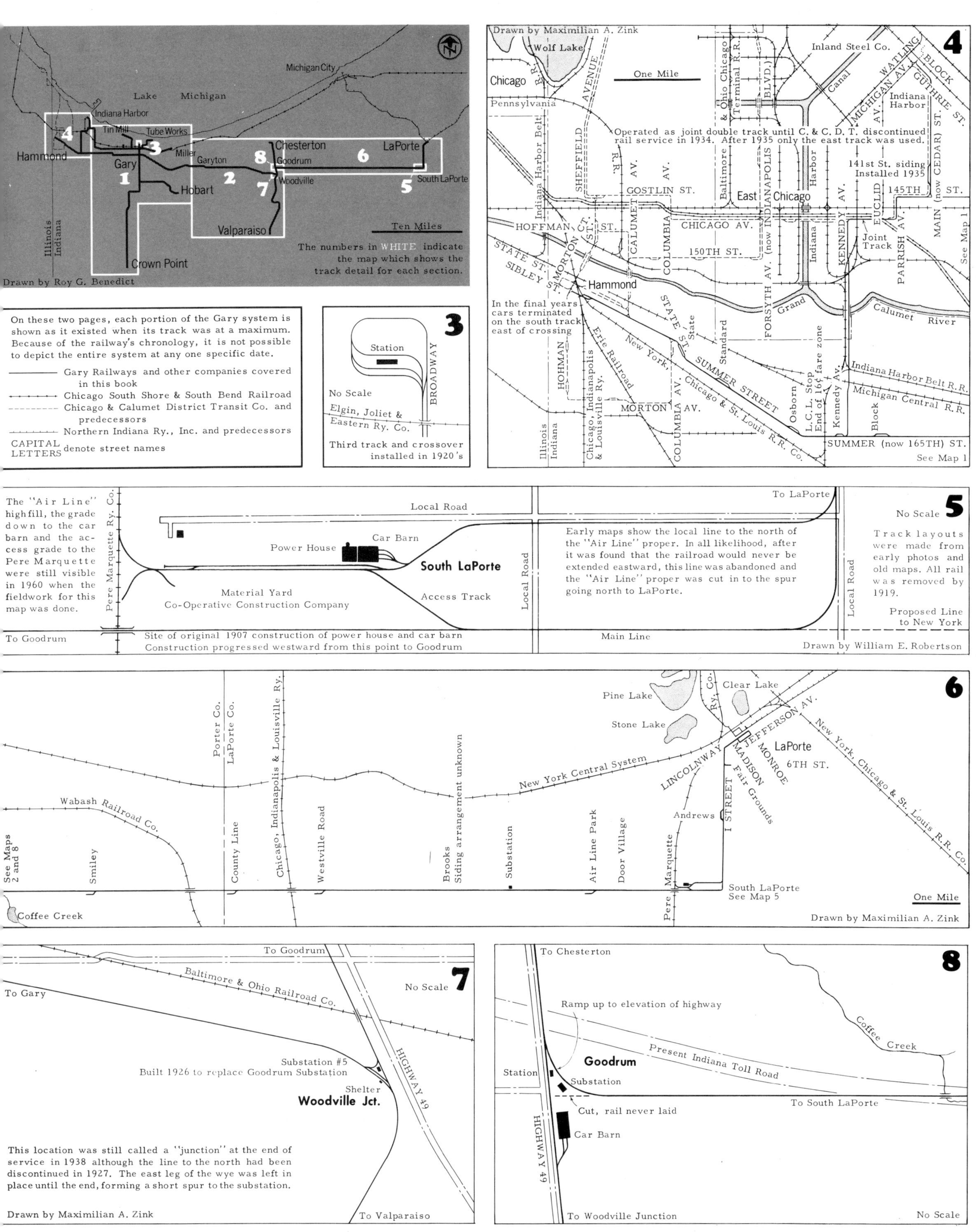

Michigan City
Lake Michigan
Indiana Harbor
Tin Mill
Tube Works
4
3
Miller
Garyton
Chesterton
LaPorte
Hammond
8
6
Goodrum
Gary
2
Woodville
1
7
Hobart
5
South LaPorte
Illinois
Indiana
Valparaiso
Crown Point
Ten Miles
The numbers in WHITE indicate
the map which shows the
track detail for each section.
Drawn by Roy G. Benedict

On these two pages, each portion of the Gary system is
shown as it existed when its track was at a maximum.
Because of the railway's chronology, it is not possible
to depict the entire system at any one specific date.

Gary Railways and other companies covered
in this book
Chicago South Shore & South Bend Railroad
Chicago & Calumet District Transit Co. and
predecessors
Northern Indiana Ry., Inc. and predecessors

CAPITAL LETTERS denote street names

3
Station
BROADWAY
No Scale
Elgin, Joliet &
Eastern Ry. Co.
Third track and crossover
installed in 1920's

4
Drawn by Maximilian A. Zink
Wolf Lake
Chicago
Inland Steel Co.
Pennsylvania
One Mile
WATLING
BLOCK
MICHIGAN AV.
GUTHRIE ST.
& O. Chicago Terminal R.R.
Indiana Harbor
Canal
AVENUE
Indiana Harbor Belt
SHEFFIELD R.R. AV.
CALUMET AV.
BALTIMORE AV.
INDIANAPOLIS (now)
Operated as joint double track until C. & C. D. T. discontinued
rail service in 1934. After 1935 only the east track was used.
GOSTLIN ST.
East Chicago
141st St. siding
Installed 1935
HOFFMAN
MORTON CT.
STATE ST.
COLUMBIA
CHICAGO AV.
Indiana
KENNEDY AV.
EUCLID
145TH
MAIN (now CEDAR) ST.
150TH ST.
See Map 1
SIBLEY ST.
STATE ST.
Joint
Track
SUMMER STREET
FORSYTH AV. (now INDIANAPOLIS)
PARRISH AV.
Hammond
Erie Railroad
New York, Chicago & St. Louis R.R. Co.
Grand
Calumet River
In the final years
cars terminated
on the south track
east of crossing
HOHMAN
Standard
Osborn
L.C.L. Stop
End of 16¢ fare zone
Kennedy Av.
Indiana Harbor Belt R.R.
HOHMAN
Chicago, Indianapolis
& Louisville Ry.
COLUMBIA AV.
Chicago & St. Louis R.R. Co.
MORTON AV.
Michigan Central R.R.
Illinois
Indiana
Block
SUMMER (now 165TH) ST.
See Map 1

5
To LaPorte
Local Road
No Scale
The "Air Line"
high fill, the grade
down to the car
barn and the ac-
cess grade to the
Pere Marquette
were still visible
in 1960 when the
fieldwork for this
map was done.
Pere Marquette Ry. Co.
Power House
Car Barn
South LaPorte
Local Road
Early maps show the local line to the north of
the "Air Line" proper. In all likelihood, after
it was found that the railroad would never be
extended eastward, this line was abandoned and
the "Air Line" proper was cut in to the spur
going north to LaPorte.
Local Road
Track layouts
were made from
early photos and
old maps. All rail
was removed by
1919.
Material Yard
Co-Operative Construction Company
Access Track
Proposed Line
to New York
To Goodrum
Site of original 1907 construction of power house and car barn
Construction progressed westward from this point to Goodrum
Main Line
Drawn by William E. Robertson

6
Pine Lake
Clear Lake
Stone Lake
JEFFERSON AV.
LaPorte
New York, Chicago & St. Louis R.R. Co.
Porter Co.
LaPorte Co.
Chicago, Indianapolis & Louisville Ry.
New York Central System
LINCOLNWAY
MADISON
MONROE
6TH ST.
Fair Grounds
Wabash Railroad Co.
County Line
Westville Road
Brooks
Siding arrangement unknown
Substation
Air Line Park
Door Village
Andrews
I STREET
Pere Marquette
See Maps 2 and 8
Smiley
South LaPorte
See Map 5
One Mile
Coffee Creek
Drawn by Maximilian A. Zink

7
To Goodrum
To Gary
Baltimore & Ohio Railroad Co.
No Scale
Substation #5
Built 1926 to replace Goodrum Substation
HIGHWAY 49
Shelter
Woodville Jct.
This location was still called a "junction" at the end of
service in 1938 although the line to the north had been
discontinued in 1927. The east leg of the wye was left in
place until the end, forming a short spur to the substation.
Drawn by Maximilian A. Zink
To Valparaiso

8
To Chesterton
Ramp up to elevation of highway
Coffee Creek
Present Indiana Toll Road
Station
Goodrum
Substation
To South LaPorte
HIGHWAY 49
Cut, rail never laid
Car Barn
To Woodville Junction
No Scale

On these two pages are replicas of operating timetables for Gary Railways interurban lines, followed by a page of public timetable replicas.

GARY RAILWAYS COMPANY — HAMMOND DIVISION — RUN NO. 1 — WESTBOUND (DAILY)

(A meet number printed above a time is shown before the time in the cell; A.M. for trips 1st–6th and 16th, P.M. for trips 7th–15th.)

STATIONS	1st	2nd	3rd	4th	5th	6th	7th	8th	9th	10th	11th	12th	13th	14th	15th	16th
LOOP		6:20	7:05	8:50	9:35	11:20	12:05	1:50	2:35	4:20	5:05	6:50	7:35	9:20	10:05	12:10
ELEVENTH AVE.	4:43	4 6:28	2 7:15	4 8:58	2-3 9:43	4 11:28	2-3 12:15	4 1:58	2-3 2:45	4 4:28	2-3 5:15	4 6:58	2-3 7:45	4-3 9:28	2-3 10:15	3-5 12:20
CHICAGO AVE.	4:53	3 6:40	3-5 7:25	3 9:10	5 9:55	3 11:40	5 12:25	3 2:10	5 2:55	3 4:40	5 5:25	3 7:10	5 7:55	5 9:40	5 10:25	2 12:30
CLARK ROAD	4:55		7:27		9:57		12:27		2:57		5:27		7:57		10:27	
WEST GARY	4:58		7:30		10:00		12:30		3:00		5:30		8:00		10:30	
IVANHOE	5:01		7:33		10:03		12:33		3:03		5:33		8:03		10:33	
KENNEDY AVE.	5:06		4 7:40		4 10:10		4 12:40		4 3:10		4 5:40		4 8:10		4 10:40	
OSBORN	5:10		7:43		10:13		12:43		3:13		5:43		8:13		10:43	
STANDARD	5:13		7:45		10:15		12:45		3:15		5:45		8:15		10:45	
STATE	5:15		7:47		10:17		12:47		3:17		5:47		8:17		10:47	
HAMMOND	5:25		7:55		10:25		12:55		3:25		5:55		8:25		10:55	

GARY RAILWAYS COMPANY — HAMMOND DIVISION — RUN NO. 5 — EASTBOUND (DAILY)

(A.M. for trips 1st–6th and 16th–17th, P.M. for trips 7th–15th.)

STATIONS	1st	2nd	3rd	4th	5th	6th	7th	8th	9th	10th	11th	12th	13th	14th	15th	16th	17th
HAMMOND		6:55		9:25		11:55		2:25		4:55		7:25		9:55			
STATE		7:01		9:31		12:01		2:31		5:01		7:31		10:01			
STANDARD		7:03		9:33		12:03		2:33		5:03		7:33		10:03			
OSBORN		7:06		9:36		12:06		2:36		5:06		7:36		10:06			
KENNEDY AVE.		4 7:10		4 9:40		4 12:10		4 2:40		4 5:10		4 7:40		4 10:10			
IVANHOE		7:15		9:45		12:15		2:45		5:15		7:45		10:15			
WEST GARY		7:18		9:48		12:18		2:48		5:18		7:48		10:18		12:05	
CLARK ROAD		7:21		9:51		12:21		2:51		5:21		7:51		10:21		12:08	
CHICAGO AVE.	5:40	1 7:25	1 8:10	1 9:55	1 10:40	1 12:25	1:10	1 2:55	3:40	1 5:25	6:10	1 7:55	8:40	1 10:25	11:10	1 12:10	12:48
ELEVENTH AVE.	2 5:51	2 7:35	2 8:21	2 10:05	2 10:51	2 12:35	2 1:21	2 3:05	2 3:51	2 5:35	2 6:21	2 8:10	2 8:51	2 10:35	2 11:21	2 12:20	2 12:55
LOOP	6:00	4 7:45	4 8:30	4 10:15	4 11:00	3 12:45	4 1:30	3 3:15	4 4:00	3 5:45	4 6:30	3 8:15	4 9:00	3 10:45	4 11:30	3 12:28	

GARY RAILWAYS COMPANY
HAMMOND DIVISION
Timetable No. A-14
Effective December 8, 1935

GARY RAILWAYS COMPANY
HAMMOND DIVISION

GENERAL TIME TABLE RULES AND INSTRUCTIONS

Gary cars operating on the Hammond Division, on their first trip out of Gary will report to the Starter at the Car Shops, giving run number, and will compare their watches with the Western Union clock in the Starter's Office.

Cars operating on the Hammond Division will operate according to Time Table, Special Instructions and Block Signal indication.

When the time is underlined, it indicates a meet on single track and the run to be met is indicated by a number above the time. A run number between times and not underlined indicates a meet on double track.

When a scheduled WESTBOUND car arrives at CHICAGO AVENUE and the Time Table shows a meet, the opposing car not having arrived and not being in the Block, the WESTBOUND car may proceed FIRST to CLARK ROAD BY getting a PERMISSIVE SIGNAL, indicating that such WESTBOUND car has properly registered IN the block.

When a scheduled WESTBOUND car arrives at KENNEDY AVENUE and the Time Table shows a meet, the opposing car not having arrived and not being in the block, the WESTBOUND car may proceed to OSBORN, under the same instructions as in paragraph above.

EASTBOUND cars arriving late at OSBORN or CLARK ROAD will expect to find a RED signal and will be governed accordingly.

In case of delays caused by car failures, accidents, fires, railroad crossing delays or other causes, the Operator will call the Starter and report the trouble, being governed by such instructions as the Starter may issue.

In foggy or stormy weather or when the visibility is obscured, all cars will be POSITIVE MEETS and under no conditions will cars be moved beyond meeting points until opposing car has arrived.

When necessary to run trains in two or more sections, the Operator of all sections but the last shall sound one long and two short whistles and the Operators of opposing cars shall answer with two short and one long whistle. Failure to receive an answer to signals for a following section must be understood to indicate that the signals have not been heard and the opposing car must be stopped and must not proceed until certain that the signals are answered and understood.

SPEED RESTRICTIONS: Positive Stops — Madison Street, Roosevelt Street, Colfax St., Kennedy Avenue, Columbia Avenue, Calumet Avenue, State Street and Oakley Avenue. In both directions and in addition to these Burr Street westbound.

Cars will reduce speed and be operated under control, sounding whistle or gong, while crossing all street intersections at which no stop is to be made to take on or discharge passengers.

Cars will approach all meeting points under full control, prepared to stop and will not exceed a speed of six miles per hour in meeting or passing any car.

Reduce speed to six miles per hour when passing under all facing switch points.

The speed of a train will ordinarily be that of its schedule, but in case of a delay no attempt will be made to make up time by reckless running. During fog or stormy weather take extraordinary precautions.

SAFETY FIRST --- ALWAYS.

34